D0279849

Understanding Documents and Sources

Edited by

Peter Catterall

and

Harriet Jones

Heinemann

Heinemann Educational Publishers
Halley Court, Jordan Hill, Oxford OX2 8EJ
a division of Reed Educational & Professional Publishing Ltd

OXFORD   MELBOURNE   AUCKLAND
JOHANNESBURG   BLANTYRE   GABORONE
IBADAN   PORTSMOUTH (NH) USA   CHICAGO

First published 1994

British Library Cataloguing in Publication Data

A catalogue record for this book is available from the British Library

ISBN 0 435 310 06 2

04 03 02 01 00 99
10 9 8 7 6 5

Typeset by TechType, Abingdon, Oxon.
Printed and bound in Great Britain by Clays Ltd, St Ives plc.

Front cover: *Rendezvous* by David Low (*Evening Standard*, 20th September 1939).

Acknowledgements

The authors and publisher would like to thank the following for the use of copyright material:

Bexley Local Studies Centre: p. 40; Centre for the Study of Cartoons and Caricature, University of Kent/Daily Mirror: p. 60 (top); Centre for the Study of Cartoons and Caricature, University of Kent/Gibberd: p. 60 (bottom); Centre for the Study of Cartoons and Caricature, University of Kent/Solo Syndication and Literary Agency: front cover, p. 59; Manchester Central Library (Local Studies Unit): p. 70 and p. 73.

Heinemann and the ICBH wish to thank all the contributors who have given permission for their work to be published in this book.

Thanks are also due to Philip Allan (Publishers) Ltd for permission to print articles which originally appeared in the *Modern History Review*

Contents

Harriet Jones
Introduction: Interpreting Documents

Harriet Jones gives a detailed introduction to the nature of and problems with using primary sources.

The teaching of history has changed considerably in the past decade, as the focus has shifted away from the use of traditional textbooks and towards the early use of primary sources. While there are many excellent survey texts available, by their very nature they set up a barrier between the student and the subject. The knowledge gained is inevitably filtered through the interpretation of the author. That is the nature of the beast, of course, and coming to an understanding of the *historiography* of a subject is an important part of the learning process. But plunging straight into the documents themselves, on the other hand, enables the student to step more directly into the past: this is at once more engaging and more challenging. It presents the student with a whole new set of problems. Traditional textbooks are comfortable, like booking a guided tour through the subject. When looking at primary sources, however, that prop is taken away.

Documentary evidence is the raw material of the historian, whose interpretation of the past is constructed through a careful sifting of many documents of varying kinds: official government records, parliamentary debates, political speeches and election manifestos, mass opinion or social surveys, diaries and memoirs, private correspondence, oral testimony, and statistical data. Increasingly, historians have had to come to terms with visual evidence as well: propaganda, cartoons, photographs, and advertisements. The aim of this book is to provide for students, confronting documentary questions, a guide to the nature, uses and pitfalls of these various types of source materials.

Approaching a document

The experienced professional historian develops her or his interpretative skills over a number of years. For the student, to be presented with a document to evaluate for the first time may seem a daunting task. The most important thing to remember is that when approaching a new piece of evidence, three questions should always be borne in mind:

- Who wrote or created the document, and for what purpose?
- When was it written or produced?
- For what audience was it created?

It follows that no piece of evidence should ever be accepted at its face value. In this sense, documents cannot be trusted to 'speak for themselves'. Rather they must be interrogated actively. The purpose of encouraging the student to read primary sources is thus to develop his or her ability to judge critically and dispassionately. This, in turn, will make it easier to understand how the argument presented by a single historian has been constructed.

Public Records

Different types of document pose their own particular problems. For example, official **government documents** from the Public Record Office (PRO) must be understood in terms of their function in the policy-making process. Policy formulation by government usually involves protracted attempts to reconcile competing interests. Discussion papers circulated in this process, generally written by civil servants, may reflect a particular stance based on economic, political or diplomatic concerns. For instance, a memorandum presented to the cabinet which argues in favour of a new policy initiative might well overstate its case in order to persuade ministers to overcome the doubts of sceptical officials in the Treasury. The byzantine machinations of Whitehall officials must never be underestimated; the history of the origins, deliberations, and consequences of the Committee on Social Insurance and Allied Services, chaired by Sir William Beveridge during the Second World War, springs to mind.

Parliamentary debates

Equally when considering **extracts from parliamentary debates,** the reader ought to be aware of the function and significance of such exchanges. Politicians asking questions, supplying answers, or debating legislation, are not necessarily simply aiming to convey factual information. Instead they may be trying to score party political points, discredit their opponents, or disguise embarrassing policy difficulties or reversals. A between-the-lines reading of the debates surrounding the Suez Crisis, for example, shows how important are those things which ministers leave unsaid. Modern parliamentary politics in Britain, in which two parties dominate, encourages a process of presentation and opposition. This sometimes lends an exaggerated impression of conflict. In reality, the gulf may not be so wide as it seems from the floor of the House of Commons. But equally, party discipline tends to stifle backbench dissent: in that case, the picture conveyed may seem consensual, when in reality there was deep disagreement.

The press

When presented with extracts from the press, the reader must consider first the editorial allegiance of the **newspaper** or **journal,** which is normally determined by the political views of the proprietor. While this may be clear enough when considering editorial commentary, straightforward press reporting of a story may be equally, if more subtly, biased for the same event can be treated wildly differently in different papers. Press coverage of identical suffragette demonstrations, for instance, are often unrecognisable as the same event. Furthermore it is sometimes the case that accurate press reporting is obstructed by forms of censorship or manipulation. That is most obviously true in times of war. But it can also be true of peacetime governments. Neville Chamberlain, for example, exercised quite ruthless control over the press corps during the years of appeasement before the Second World War. A less obvious consideration is the way in which press coverage is commonly used as evidence by the historian. A regular pitfall is to assume that the press reflects public opinion, whereas in fact it may be attempting to shape it.

Public surveys

Information on public attitudes is easier to judge when consideration of press coverage is supplemented by data gathered from **social surveys, professional opinion pollsters**, or **marketing research companies**. The early social surveys, such as those conducted by Charles Booth in London or Seebohm Rowntree in York, have long been relied upon by economic and social historians of the Edwardian period, and accompanied by other social surveys conducted in subsequent decades, help to measure the degree and extent of poverty at different periods in time with a reasonable degree of accuracy. Since the Second World War, when Mass Observation analyses became an important factor in helping the government to determine the state of public morale, evidence collected in this fashion has grown far more varied and sophisticated. After the war, when the development of an age of mass consumerism made it much more important for businesses to gauge the market accurately, there was an explosion of this type of information gathering for the use of private industry. Thus we now have a new and rich source of evidence from which political, economic and social historians may draw, on issues as diverse as voting intentions and men's shaving habits.

Personal accounts

Evidence from public surveys is important in explaining the attitudes of large numbers of people. But our understanding of reactions to events can be enriched further by the personal accounts of participants in or witnesses to historical events. **Diaries, memoirs,** and **oral testimony,** of course, cannot be expected to be wholly objective. A diary entry, for example, may be simply the immediate response to a day's events, written from a personal perspective which is subject to change. Many diarists do not write in this way, however. Often a diary is reconstructed weeks after the event, and it is not always made clear to the reader whether or not this is the case. Some diarists consciously write for subsequent publication, a factor which may lead them to be selective in their version of events in a way which would not apply to a diary not originally intended for publication.

The problem of assessing memoirs or oral testimony is somewhat different. Here, recollections are affected by the passage of time, the application of hindsight to justify one's own record and possible lapses of memory, commonly leading to the conflation of events. This means that such sources should not be relied upon exclusively, although they can reveal important background influences which may help to explain the position adopted by an individual, and give some indication of the context in which events unfolded. It is important to remember, however, that individual recollections of the same event can vary enormously. The recent spate of memoirs which has emerged from the Thatcher years illustrates this point well.

Private papers and correspondence can give valuable glimpses into the true motives or opinion of individuals, which may be unclear from the official records. On a different level, **letters** can indeed be a marvellous source of information on personal life and social mores for the social historian. Of course, letters are written to a known and specific individual. The same author may disclose quite different views to other acquaintances or to a wider audience.

Statistics

Economic and demographic **statistics** can seem a misleadingly straightforward source of information. For one thing, statistics are only collected for specific purposes, and consistent and reliable sources of information on seemingly simple issues can be impossible to find. For example, historians continue to argue over the movement of working-class incomes in the Edwardian period, and put forward a bewildering array of formulas for adjusting available statistics accurately. Historians and students of post-war immigration into Britain have a similarly difficult task, as statistical data was simply not collected thoroughly for many years. So when approaching the raw data which are available, it is important to establish why the statistics were collected in the first place and to understand the purpose for which they were used at the time. Because the weight of such evidence may appear on the surface to be irrefutable, statistical data can be used to lend credence to otherwise questionable assertions.

Visual evidence

The same themes which arise when considering written forms of evidence can be applied to visual images. Questions of authorship, intention, date of origin and audience should be addressed to the same degree. Political propaganda, of course, has an obvious audience in the electorate, and its intention is fairly clear. **Cartoons** can be used to put forward an editorial point of view; a single dramatic image can indeed perform that task more effectively than several column inches of text. In the works of Illingsworth, Partridge, Strube, Low, Vicky and Zec – to name but a few – British historians of the twentieth century have a rich field of political cartoonists from which to draw. **Advertisements,** because they are intended to persuade the audience at which they are aimed by tapping their concerns, can provide important clues to the period in which they were launched.

No one pretends that the interpretation of historical evidence is a simple task. But it would be patronising to leave that job only to the professional historian. Presenting primary material to students of history at a relatively early stage has important repercussions. For it is only through direct experience of interpretation and analysis that one can come to understand the process by which history is written. As the national curriculum in history develops, the demand for documents-based textbooks is expanding. Many new series of this type have come on the market. They are not intended to replace the standard and well-thumbed secondary accounts. But by increasing the accessibility of primary resources in history, students are being encouraged to make their own judgements.

Harriet Jones is the author (with Lawrence Butler) of *Britain in the Twentieth Century: a Documentary Reader* **(Heinemann, 1994).**

John W. Young
Diplomatic Documents

Diplomatic historians are more affected than most by restrictions on access to documents. This problem and the ways of dealing with available documents is discussed here.

Over the last century the governments of the major powers have invested large sums in producing their own volumes of diplomatic documents. This in itself is unusual, in that foreign policy seems to be the only area of government in which historical documents are produced on a substantial scale. Why should foreign ministries employ a staff of historians, as well as archivists, to produce 'official' histories and documents collections? In some cases the reason is simple: in the era of growing democracy and world wars each power wishes to defend its own case – to its own people and foreigners – in the arguments leading to major conflicts. This for example seems to be the main reason why the French government has produced three series of documents in the past on the background to the wars of 1870, 1914 and 1939. The French, in short, have hoped to demonstrate that they were not primarily responsible for any of these conflicts. After 1945 the Allies, however, captured German archives and were able to produce many volumes – in English – which helped to illuminate Hitler's expansionism of the 1930s.

There are other cases where a particular historical debate led to documents being published. In the United States for example there was intense criticism after the war of President Roosevelt's 'surrender' of Eastern Europe to Stalin's Soviet Union at the 1945 Yalta conference. As a result the Americans published a volume of documents on the conference as part of that official series of documents, *Foreign Relations of the United States*. Unfortunately, as well as containing revelations about Soviet expansionism, this volume included some unflattering references to General de Gaulle, the wartime French leader. In 1958 de Gaulle returned to power in France, his resentment of American domination having been strengthened by these revelations. However, most of the volumes in *Foreign Relations of the United States* (which cover the period since 1919) have little to do with specific historical debates.

British documents

In Britain the government too has defended its case in world affairs, and particularly in relation to major conflicts, by publishing series of documents. The volumes on the interwar years, *Documents on British Foreign Policy,* were particularly lengthy and full, covering all subjects from the international conferences attended by Lloyd George after the First World War to the rise of aggressive states in Europe and East Asia in the 1930s, but taking in such detailed subjects *en route* as the establishment of the Baltic states and the complexities of Balkan politics. The Second World War itself is covered by a considerable number of official histories – including Sir Llewellyn Woodward's history of foreign policy – but no documents. In the post-war years however the Foreign Office historians have (since 1984) joined a field where previously the Americans were dominant. Spending restrictions mean that the new collections will not be as full as the interwar volumes, but two series are being produced. The first, on the years 1945–50 already includes volumes on the 1945 Potsdam conference, atomic issues and events in Germany, whilst a second series deals with 1950–51 and such issues as German rearmament and the dawn of European unity.

These volumes mean, to take one example, that historians now have documents on the Potsdam conference available from all three powers involved – America, Britain and Russia – although the Soviet documents, published in English in 1959 (as *The Conferences of Tehran, Malta and Potsdam*) are little more than minutes of the principal meetings, and not very revealing. The American and British volumes include such documents as:

- records of the three-power meetings;
- copies of the agreements reached;
- records of any special meetings – for example between two of the powers present;
- 'briefing papers', prepared as background for delegates at a conference;
- important minutes and memoranda written by officials and ministers during the conference;
- significant telegrams received from embassies around the world at the time.

This is typical of the US and British documentary volumes: an attempt is made to produce a wide selection of materials on the most important aspects of an issue. One advantage that the official historians have over other researchers is access to a wider range of materials. The post-1945 *Documents on British Policy Overseas* for example includes documents which are not yet available at the Public Record Office, because of government secrecy restrictions.

On the other hand it must be emphasised that the published volumes are only a *selection* of materials. Those who wish to see the full range of minutes, memoranda, telegrams, meetings and agreements which are available on British foreign policy must travel to the Record Office at Kew. A number of private papers collections, including those of several Foreign Secretaries, also exist there. Major speeches and international agreements will already exist in published form.

Problems of international history

Diplomatic history, it is true, used to be treated as a narrow field of research: diplomacy was simply 'what one state said to another' and was viewed as a rather closed, dull field – even if it helped to explain why international disagreements could spill over into global war. But over the past few decades international historians have begun to look beyond the dry diplomatic exchanges, to examine the national aspirations which underlie them, the social make-up and education of the principle policy-makers and how their decisions could be affected, in democratic societies, by popular demands, parliamentary and press criticisms and party-political considerations. Clearly, in Britain in the 1930s for example, popular reluctance to face another war (reflected in the famous Oxford Union debate), combined with opposition to crude power-politics (seen in the outrage caused by British plans to give much of Abyssinia to Mussolini) had an important impact on Chamberlain's policy of appeasement. Other factors which need to be taken into consideration in studying diplomacy however include:

- defence capabilities – has a country got the military power to back a strong foreign policy?
- the use of propaganda – how does a state defend its case and manipulate opinion in its favour?
- the activities of the intelligence agencies – of particular interest in the twentieth century with the emergence of MI6, the CIA, the KGB and the like.

To give justice to all these elements means looking at an ever-wider range of evidence. But the mention of defence, propaganda and intelligence matters raises the problems of obtaining the evidence. Governments may be keen to defend their case in international contexts, but this in itself means that they may be selective about which documents they are ready to produce. At the Public Record Office it is extremely difficult to reconstruct the history of intelligence work, atomic weapons development or the use of propaganda. Although historians like Christopher Andrew (with intelligence) or Philip M. Taylor (with propaganda) have shown what can be achieved, and although official histories have been produced on intelligence work in the Second World War and on atomic developments, the bulk of material on these areas remains 'closed', even after several decades. This adds to the problems faced not just by international historians but by all historians, even in an area so abundant in evidence as twentieth-century Britain. There are always lost documents, major political figures who have left no private papers, important meetings left unrecorded, documents withheld because they include something of a 'personal' nature, and pieces of evidence which directly contradict each other. Taken together these factors help to ensure that historical debates will always continue, and radical disagreements will arise, even on such well-worn subjects as the outbreak of war in 1914 and the meaning of appeasement. Then again, with subjects as important as national survival and global conflict it is only right that the interest in them should be deep, the answers put forward controversial, the debate between historians intense.

John W. Young is Professor of Politics at the University of Leicester.

B. R. Mitchell

Statistics

Statistics are frequently used to assess, for instance, economic performance or military strength. But how reliable are they and how can historians avoid the pitfalls involved in their interpretation?

At one time students were often encouraged to study history because they were 'not much good at maths'. Apart from the obvious condemnation of this attitude on the grounds that one should have a positive reason for one's chosen field of study, it was not even readily defensible on its own negative ground. Except possibly in very narrow fields, no historian can avoid numbers and numerical concepts. Numbers figure prominently in the military history of all ages; in any account of parliaments; in demographic and other aspects of social history; and of course, in the most obvious field, economic history. Moreover, any attempts to assess the significance of different historical influences in terms of more or less importance are implicitly concerned with concepts of quantity. Even in trivial matters, numbers properly interpreted may make a different impression from numbers casually used. A fine illustration of this was quoted by Donald McCloskey[1] from Boswell's biography of Dr Johnson:

Boswell: Sir Alexander Dick tells me that he remembers having a thousand people in a year to dine at his house...

Johnson: That, Sir, is about three a day.

Boswell: How your statement lessens the idea.

Johnson: That, Sir, is the good of counting. It brings everything to a certainty which before floated in the mind indefinitely.

Admittedly, the numbers with which military historians are directly concerned usually involve only simple arithmetic; but behind the armies – and the diplomats, too – lie their recruitable populations and their logistical support, that is the economic power which their governmental masters can command. And once historians have to consider economies and finances, they are of necessity dealing in many kinds of numbers and their complex relationships with one another. In other words, they have to contend with statistics – numerical facts, systematically categorised and analysed – and if they are to understand what they have to say, they must at least have a nodding acquaintance with their provenance and limitations, and be capable of a scepticism that is discriminating rather than stultifying.

Statistical sources

There are many kinds of sources of historical statistics and it is scarcely possible here to do more than refer to a few of them. At the level of national aggregates, the vast majority are to be found in the archives and official publications of governments and, for the twentieth century, of international organisations such as the League of Nations, the United Nations Organisation, and their offshoots. This applies to statistics of population, the workforce, industries and their production, trade, finances, education, crime, invention, land ownership, and a host of other subjects. National governmental publications are a major source, also, for statistics of local government units, though these often publish their own data separately. Some associations connected with major industries and services also produce aggregative statistical data. Finally – and probably most usefully for the historian with no ambitions for deep statistical analysis – collections of historical statistics are now available for a number of countries.[2] At the level of the individual firm, most business records, even ancient ones, contain some kinds of statistical material. For political statistics the official records of legislatures are useful, and so are the newspapers and journals of the period.

Imperfections in data

Virtually all statistical data are subject to errors in collection and presentation, and in some cases there may be deliberate misrepresentation or outright falsification. However, there is no reason to suppose that this was any worse in the past than at present. From time to time enumerators make slips, printers make errors, businesses suppress or falsify information and governments do the same on a grander scale. But this is no reason for failing to use the data which have been provided. Much can be done with imperfect data, either because rough approximation is enough to point to particular conclusions, or because sophisticated techniques can be used to assess and control the margins of error. The historian has the same need as any other student to be on guard, and weigh the likelihood of error in the evidence, be it numerical or otherwise, and the size of its possible effect on any conclusions drawn.

Though the statistics of the past are not necessarily more prone to error than those of today, some of the sources of error may well be met with more commonly in historical data than in those of our own day. Any time series of statistics is subject to changes in definition or in breadth of coverage which are not obvious in the sources, but awareness of this possibility has certainly grown as statistics have been more systematically used. The external trade statistics of many countries have notoriously been prone to such changes. A related, and often less easily-perceived problem, is the existence of data from different sources which may seem to relate to the same thing, but which do not in fact do so. International comparisons are particularly subject to this snare. Again, the efficiency of collectors and compilers of statistics may well be imperfect today just as in the past, but there are more checks on them nowadays, and there are better techniques for assessing their effectiveness (such as post-censal sampling to estimate the extent of census omissions). For historical data there are usually no ways of knowing what variations took place in compiler's accuracy, and if much depends on this, the historians must, as always, stick to their duty to weigh the evidence. Deliberate falsification is another matter, and there is plenty to suggest that this problem, so far as it relates to governments' actions, has become worse in some countries in recent times. Often there is little or nothing that the historian can do about unknown variability in validity of data, though deliberate falsification may be revealed in time. Even before then it may be possible to make approximate estimates of the 'genuine' numbers. (Various western estimates of economic aggregates for the Soviet Union from the 1930s to the 1960s are examples of this process.)

Peculiar problems of historical statistics

So far we have been mainly concerned with problems of statistical data in general, rather than those which are peculiar to historical statistics. Some purists might argue that there are none of these; but most would accept that, in practice, they do exist. The main ones of this kind are those of missing or inadequate data – either the absence of some numbers which 'should' be known but which have not survived the passage of time and are simply not in the historical record; or the complete absence of numbers which historians would like to have. These latter often result from the fact that people in earlier periods did not think in the same way or in terms of the same categories as modern historians. It may also arise because it was no-one's business to record certain data. The notorious paucity of information on retail prices before the end of the nineteenth century is a case in point.

The sporadic absence of certain numbers in a statistical series may not always matter very much – the destruction by fire of the British Customs records for 1813 hardly affects conclusions about the course of overseas trade in the Napoleonic Wars, for example. But if more than the occasional figure is missing, a much greater degree of uncertainty may be introduced. It is then that the historian may have to have recourse to the expertise of the theoretical statistician, either to estimate the missing numbers or to assess the margin of error which their absence occasions. This is not usually of much help, however, in dealing with those problems which arise because, prior to the end of the nineteenth century, few national statistical data exist which were collected for their own sake. Most were by-products of taxation or military-preparedness, and in both these case there may well have been a premium on evading inclusion. Normally all the historian can do is to accept that these data are imperfect and qualify any conclusions which are drawn in an appropriate fashion.

Common statistical traps

Three further snares which sometimes trap historians, particularly those who are not economic historians but who wish to advert to economic changes, are worth special mention here. The first is the ease with which percentages may mislead the historian as well as his or her readers if no account is taken of the absolute size of the base from which they are taken. This is analogous to the trap which Dr Johnson sprung on Boswell. A 1000% rise in (say) Bulgarian steel output over five years may seem huge and highly significant – until it is pointed out that the initial output was minute. The second is somewhat similar – namely the casual use of a number without proper definition and without any attempt to indicate whether it is 'big' or 'small'. An example of this occurs in Okey's excellent introductory history of Eastern Europe since the mid-eighteenth century, when he writes:

'Despite repression and mass emigration the intelligentsia of the Congress Kingdom still grew from 7,500 to 11,700 members between 1830 and 1863'.

Who are his intelligentsia and how big are the numbers relative to the total Polish population or to similarly-defined people in other countries? Without these pieces of information the numbers really mean nothing.[3]

Finally, there is the notorious index number problem, full explanation of which is beyond the scope of this article. There are actually several such problems, but the one of which historians need most to be aware is that an index which accurately reflects the composition of some variable – say the cost-of-living – in any one year will not, in a world of changing tastes, incomes, prices and products, have precisely the right weighting of items consumed in another year. Changing the weights and linking separate indexes is one solution to this problem, but it takes away exact precision of comparability between years. Such precision can, of course, become meaningless if some commodities composing an index cease to be consumed and others take their place. For example, a cost-of-living index which included candles but not electricity would not be of much use today. All worthwhile indices, therefore, have to be compromises between relevance and precision in comparison, and the historian should never forget this.

Notes

(1) McLoskey, D.N. *Econometric History* (1987) p. 42.

(2) Too numerous to list here, references to most can be found in Mitchell, B.R. *International Historical Statistics* (1975–83) 3 Vols.

(3) Of course it is unfair of me to pick on Okey's book for there are many more – and worse – offenders. I happened to be reading that particular book at the time of writing this article.

B.R. Mitchell is a Fellow of Trinity College, Cambridge, and a recently retired University Lecturer in Economics.

Brian Brivati
Private Papers

Private papers are amongst the most valuable of historical documents but they can require particular sensitivity in their use. Brian Brivati concentrates on the papers of political figures.

Anyone who does not feel excited by the prospect of sitting in an archive waiting for invariably brown folders, contained in box files and tied up by irritating pieces of ribbon, should not consider becoming an historian. Part of the excitement for the historian dealing with private papers is the way, especially with large collections of correspondence, archivists combine an extended period together in one file and hidden treasure can appear slipped between the most mundane of letters.

Collections of private papers are the basic building blocks used in the writing of many different genres of history. They are almost indispensable in writing biographies; they provide the individual's perspective on institutional and party political history and small, seemingly irrelevant, papers of private individuals can offer unique insights into ordinary lives for the social and local historian.

Papers and personal insights

Dr Angela Raspin, the archivist of the London School of Economics, defined private papers in an excellent essay on the subject:

> Private documents accumulated by, belonging to, and subject to the disposition of an individual person ... Private papers are the physical survivals of a life. A politician's papers contain correspondence with family and personal friends and political colleagues, minutes and notes on informal meetings, drafts of policy papers, formal correspondence and official papers retained from periods of office. Unless the originator kept copies of his letters or asked for the originals back, his papers will contain only letters written to him.[1]

Each of the different parts of private collections that Dr Raspin identifies illustrates the problems and possibilities inherent in the use of private papers. Most of the important collections are fully catalogued and have been used by researchers in the past, although each brings his own particular research priorities and finds fascinating that which others have passed over. Occasionally an historian has the opportunity to examine a stash of papers which have not been looked at before or have not yet been catalogued. Each document becomes a voyage of discovery and the remarkable thing is that there is still so much to discover.

The personal papers of a political figure, those relating to their private lives, family and friends, can offer otherwise inaccessible insights into hidden sides of public lives. Where it has not been edited out, much of this part of a collection can be concerned with commonplace and everyday details with which we all at one time of our lives will have to deal; buying houses; organising children's education; coping with illness and death and financial matters. These can reveal aspects of the person's personality not seen in public activity. For example the papers of the nuclear disarmer Philip Noel-Baker contain correspondence on his interest in alternative medicine and those of the Trade Union leader Bill Carron contain swathes of sympathy letters sent to him after his heart attack and details of his involvement with the Roman Catholic Church.

A subjective source

Correspondence with political colleagues falls into two broad categories; those written with a view to the future and those which are genuinely private. Many of the latter never reach the historian. In the case of the former, some political figures have both eyes on the future. Selwyn Lloyd, the Conservative foreign secretary at the time of Suez, was particularly keen on having a biography written about him and wrote at the end of his life, 'I have done my best to sort out my papers and leave them in as convenient form as possible for anyone who wishes to take the trouble to look at them'.[2] Others, like Iain Mikardo the maverick left-wing Labour MP, were not so concerned with the future and looked with a slight disapproval on their colleagues that were. In his memoirs be recorded his views on one of the famous Labour diarists:

> Barbara Castle used to write furiously right though every committee meeting she attended, simultaneously recording the proceedings and taking an active part in them. We all greatly admired her capacity to be in two places at once: writing down what one of her colleagues was saying and at the same time working out what she was going to say in reply. It must have been pretty wearing.'[3]

Committing opinions, analysis and future plans of action to paper can offer hostages to fortune. This highlights the central problem of private papers; they are, by definition, one of the most subjective of sources and are often edited by their subjects. One of the most frustrating experiences a researcher can have is finding a reference to a letter which is not in the collection of the writer or the recipient. Even worse are the occasions when the entry in a guide like Chris Cook's *Sources in British Political History 1900–1951*, reads: 'Clough, Sir Robert (1873–1965) MP (Con) Keighley 1918–1922. At the request of his widow all his diaries and papers were destroyed.'[4]

Some official papers find themselves in private papers. Restrictions on retaining official papers have been circumvented by cabinet ministers who simply kept papers issued by the cabinet secretary which should have been returned. These papers, when they are found among private papers, provide one of the chinks in the armour of the thirty year rule and the Official Secrets Act. Even Prime Ministers have been guilty of this high-level pilfering; Churchill and Lloyd George were particularly prone to this.

A sidelight to official papers or committee minutes and other documents are the notes, remarks, or in Clement Attlee's case, doodles, which politicians made during long, and often boring, meetings. These excursions can bring a flash of humanity or a clue to the mood of the people at the time. During the press conference to launch the Campaign for Democratic Socialism in 1960, Bill Rodgers wrote in bold capitals across the top of his briefing notes 'Forces of Sanity'.

Some politicians are extremely diligent about writing notes on important conversations or recording their impression on particular important events. This is partly an exercise in organising their thinking on the questions of the day. But it is also done with a view to the writing of their memoirs. This diligence can be especially useful when the politician concerned does not keep a diary. Roy Jenkins for example used his own aides-mémoire, written while Chancellor of the Exchequer, in the composition of his memoirs.

The decline of letter-writing

Occasionally the sheer volume of material contained in a private collection, especially if a politician had a long career, can be daunting. David Dilks recounted in his preface to *Neville Chamberlain*, 'Mr Iain Macleod embarked on a fresh account [of Chamberlain's life], but groaned on being handed seven large boxes of papers, and wondered "Whether it was necessary to read them all".'[5] The size of collections is particularly apparent for nineteenth-century political figures. The golden age of political letter-writing was the reign of Queen Victoria, with the monarch leading the pack. In the Gladstone papers alone there are 577 letters and 141 telegrams from the Queen. 'At the time of the Egyptian Campaign in 1882 one day alone brought 17 letters from the Queen or her private secretary to the Secretary of State for War.'[6] The Victorian predilection for letter-writing probably found its highest form in the prose of Benjamin Disraeli. The classic example quoted in Robert Blake's biography is Disraeli's letter to his wife Mary Ann. One passage gives the flavour of much of his style:

> As a woman of the world, which you are thoroughly, you ought not, you cannot be, unacquainted with the difference that subsists between our relative position. The continuance of the present state of affairs could only render you disreputable, me it renders infamous. There is only one construction which society, & justly, puts upon a connection between a woman who is supposed to be rich & a man whom she avowedly loves & does not marry. In England especially there is no stigma more damning; it is one which no subsequent conduct or position ever permits to be forgotten. It has crushed men who have committed with impunity even crimes; some things may indeed be more injurious, none more ignominious.[7]

Such eloquence may now take place down telephone lines and will be lost to the historian. However the increasing popularity of the fax machine may help to alleviate this loss of written records somewhat.

Problems of access

To an extent control of the way historians will analyse a period lies with the way politicians deal with their private papers. Perceptions of certain episodes can be formed by the completeness of the record kept by an individual. Perceptions of the Conservative Party's rethink of the late 1940s and early 1950s have been influenced by the completeness of Rab Butler's papers. Posthumous control can also be exerted by restricting access to private papers to official biographers: Philip Williams' monopoly of Hugh Gaitskell, Martin Gilbert's of Winston Churchill and Philip Ziegler's of Harold Wilson are obvious examples. The executor of the politician's estate is responsible for depositing papers in a holding institution like Churchill College, Cambridge or the British Library, and can place any restrictions on the time to elapse before the papers are open or limit the parts of the collection that are open for researchers, that they desire. While this is understandable in the case of politicians still living or when family or colleagues might be embarrassed by the revelations contained in the papers, or indeed when the Official Secrets Act might be broken, these restrictions can leave gaps in the historical record. Or they can leave students, historians and general readers overly reliant on favourably disposed 'official' histories.

Balance and selection

The researcher using private papers must sometimes enter into negotiations with the executors of the politician's estate. Some executors see themselves as the defenders of historical reputations and may undertake the job of biography themselves. Few would dispute Michael Foot's place as public defender of the memory of Aneurin Bevan. In other instances it is the historian who makes the critical judgements. The balance of how much to disclose must be defined by offsetting the potential benefit to historians of revealing private information against the pain such disclosure would cause. The public actions of public figures deserve full disclosure. The private actions of public figures must be weighed up more carefully. Robert Rhodes James defined the balancing act perfectly in discussing which aspects of Bob Boothby's private life he decided to include in his recent biography of the Conservative politician:

> It is always difficult for the political biographer to achieve the right balance between the public and private life, but it was notably difficult in Boothby's case. His long romance with Dorothy Macmillan had a profound political and personal significance; other affairs did not and so I have been reticent about them. I know the circumstances, but have chosen not to reveal them as this would cause quite unnecessary pain to several people; they are also not relevant to the story of Boothby's life. He, too, would have been shocked and distressed if these matters were broadcast. I have exercised a similar discretion in the past, for which I make no apology. One day all may be revealed, but not by me and certainly not now.[8]

As Rhodes James points out, the real task is to decide what contribution disclosure will be making to understanding the subject. The issue also raises questions about what constitutes 'private' and 'public'. Our understanding of these terms has evolved:

> The first recorded uses of the 'public' in English identify the 'public' with common good in society ... later, there was added a sense of 'public' as that which is manifest and open to general observation. Hall wrote in his *Chronicle* of 1542, 'Their inward grudge could not refrayne but crys out in places publicke and also private.' 'Private' was here used to mean privileged, at a high governmental level. By the end of the seventeenth century, the opposition of 'public' and 'private' was shaded more like the way the terms are now used. 'Public' meant open to scrutiny of anyone, whereas 'private' meant a sheltered reign of life defined by one's family and friends.[9]

Private papers represent one of the few area were the rigid separation between public and private is broken down and a sense of the whole of a public life can be glimpsed.

The problems presented to historians concerning the volume of material, overcoming restrictions of access, balancing the public and the private and keeping in the forefront of one's mind the subjectivity of a person's private papers, are obviously minor when set against the value of a private collection. At the end of a good day working in an archive one has a set of index cards covered in pencilled notes and a feeling that one has stepped for a brief moment into the 'physical survivals' of somebody else's life.

Notes

(1) Raspin Angela, 'Private Papers'. Seldon A. (ed.) *Contemporary History, Practice and Method* (Basil Blackwell, 1988) pp. 89–101.
(2) Quoted in Thorpe, D.R. *Selwyn Lloyd* (Cape, 1989) p. xv.
(3) Mikardo, I. *Back-Bencher* (Weidenfeld and Nicolson, 1988) pp. 1–2.
(4) Cook, C. *Sources in British Political History 1900–1951, Volume 3: A Guide to Private Papers of Members of Parliament, A-K* and *Volume 4: L-Z*, (Macmillan) p. 93.
(5) Dilks, D. *Neville Chamberlain, Volume One: Pioneering and Reform, 1869–1929*, (Cambridge University Press, 1984) p. ix.
(6) Hardie, F. *The Political Influence of the Monarchy 1868–1952* (1970) p. 2.
(7) Blake, R. *Disraeli* (Methuen, 1966) p. 769.
(8) Rhodes James, R. *Bob Boothby: A Portrait* (Macmillan, 1991) p. 14.
(9) Sennett, R. (1977) *The Fall of Public Man* (Faber and Faber, 1977) p. 16.

Brian Brivati lectures in History at the University of Kingston.

Peter Catterall
Oral History

Oral history is a source which is inceasingly used in 'A' level projects. But how useful, and reliable, is it?

The interviewing of patients in geriatric wards about their youth and experiences is now used as a way of helping these patients to retain both their dignity and their faculties. This is a valuable therapeutic exercise. There remain, however, many historians who doubt whether any type of oral history can have much historical, as opposed to therapeutic, value.

Oral history has indeed been dismissed as being little better than conversations with geriatrics. A.J.P. Taylor most famously remarked that all it gives us is 'old men drooling about their youth'.[1] Such scepticism has not, however, prevented an increasing use of oral sources by historians of the late nineteenth and twentieth centuries in recent years. Historical documentaries on television in particular rely heavily on sources which have some visual impact, such as the interview or the newsreel. Historians have never been slaves of a single source material. Although historical writing in a sense can only begin in a situation where there is a written record on which to base an analysis, it does not necessarily have to end there.

All research requires careful evaluation of the evidence. Oral sources have, however, been seen as particularly unreliable. For instance, David Marquand, in interviews for his biography of the first Labour Prime Minister, Ramsay MacDonald, found 'Memories amazingly short and amazingly fallible'.[2] They are particularly flawed when it comes to specifics, such as dates, names or sequences of events. Even good memories can prove partial, in both senses of the word. The interviewee may, of course, set out to falsify and mislead, but this is less of a problem than unintentional inaccuracy. Among the potential problems resulting are over-simplification of events viewed from a personal perspective or an exaggeration of his own or his organisation's role in these events. Friendships, animosities and partisanship can also distort an interviewee's testimony: for example, an interviewee asked about his friends' actions is likely to be charitable, even if he remembers feeling rather differently at the time.

The methods employed by interviewees can also contribute to the perceived unreliability of oral sources. An unrepresentative sample of interviewees can, for instance, seriously distort the picture that emerges. The construction and selection of the questions can also distort the evidence produced by an interview. This can lead to incomplete evidence, because the follow-up questions to exhaust the interviewee's knowledge on the subject went unasked. It can also easily lead to the interviewer hearing only what he wants to hear, because of the selection and construction of the sentences. This can best be combated by approaching the same subject from a variety of angles, in order to offer the interviewee the opportunity of looking at it in a number of ways, and, incidentally, to test his powers of recall.

The same approach should be used to guard against the related problem of the interviewee trying to tell his interrogator what he thinks he wants to know. This can even result in the quite misleading impression that he knows all there is to know on a subject. It should, however, be remembered that interviewees' memories may be limited simply because their knowledge was limited. For instance, the secrets of 'Ultra', the British success in breaking the German codes during the Second World War, were unknown outside of a small circle, and no amount of questioning of those outside the circle was likely to produce any knowledge of the affair.

Perhaps the most important of the criticisms of oral sources is that they have none of the contemporaneity of other historical sources, such as letters, diaries, documents or official reports. All of these latter sources suffer to some extent from selectivity but they do not suffer the additional selectivity of memory. Hindsight brings further problems. It is not just that, as Philip Williams noted, 'Politicians subconsciously adapt their views about the past to fit a stance they had adopted later'.[3] With the encouragement of their interviewers, witnesses may dwell on the subjects that seem important in historical context, without necessarily recapturing the other issues and considerations that seemed important at the time.

These objections perhaps apply particularly to the interviewing of important people (which has become known as élite oral history), rather than to the well-established use of oral sources in the field of social history. It is indeed from political, diplomatic and defence historians that the strongest opposition has come. These historians rely more than most on special documentary evidence. Even so, some of the best oral archives in Britain, of which there is an excellent example in the field of military history at the Imperial War Museum, have been built up by those working in these fields. This material, suitably checked, can flesh out the rather dry picture that emerges from the documents. It should be remembered that much business is now transacted on the telephone and is in danger of passing unrecorded. It has indeed been said that history could only be written properly for the twenty years between the invention of the typewriter and the telephone, for the one greatly increased the number and legibility of documents preserved and the other meant that an increasing amount went unrecorded. Record-keeping anyway is often less thorough than historians would wish. The early tapping of memories is an important way of remedying these defects.

Interviews can also help to recapture relationships, the all-important who knew whom and who influenced whom, and procedures. At the same time interviews can help to recreate the atmosphere of a situation or period. This is indeed particularly what they are used for by social historians. Oral testimony provides valuable evidence of social attitudes and behaviour. It is also often the only way to recapture people's experiences. For instance, the work of the Bradford Heritage Recording Unit in recording the experience of immigrants in their city is providing a resource bank unparalleled in any documentary collection. Similar oral history projects have proved invaluable in recording vanishing crafts and vanishing lifestyles. An example is the collection on the changing life and work of the East Anglian fisherman c1890–c1930 at the Maritime Museum for East Anglia, Great Yarmouth.

For these reasons, oral history seems to have been more readily accepted by social historians than by those working in other fields. Another reason may be that some of the objections to oral history do not apply with the same force when it is used in this way. Social historians tend to be looking for evidence about attitudes and behaviour rather than seeking to reconstruct in great detail specific events. In most cases, therefore, the material they are looking for is of a general kind less subject to the vagaries of memory. The relatively large numbers of people interviewed in these cases can also facilitate the checking of the veracity of this oral material.

The use of such oral evidence can help to illuminate areas which are not covered by the documents. This is true not only for social historians but also for trade union, political or church historians, all of whom can find the records of the organisations they are studying frustratingly terse, especially at the local level. And oral history can add to the record for those working in other fields as well. For instance, in scientific history Nicholas Kurti found that 'in scientific research the false starts are very often not recorded in contemporary documentation',[4] being only discovered in the course of interviews.

In summary, then, interviews are a somewhat unreliable source and oral evidence should be used with caution. Nevertheless, much useful material can be gained from oral sources to supplement, and in cases in lieu of, documentary evidence. Even the reminiscences of the geriatric ward can , as John Adams points out, 'recreate a world we have lost, and if they are not reliable in every respect they at least help us to furnish the milieu from which the patients came'.[5]

Notes

(1) Quoted in Harrison, B. 'Oral history and recent political history', *Oral History* 3 (1972) p. 46.

(2) Cited in Seldon, A. and Pappworth, J. *By Word of Mouth* (Methuen, 1983) p. 17.

(3) Williams, P. 'Interviewing politicians', *Political Quarterly* 51/3 (1980) p. 311.

(4) Cited in Seldon and Pappworth, op. cit., p. 38.

(5) Adams, J. 'Reminiscences in the geriatric ward: an undervalued resource', *Oral History* 12/2 (1984) pp. 57–8.

Peter Catterall is Director of the Institute of Contemporary British History, Visiting Lecturer in History at Queen Mary and Westfield College, London and editor of the *Modern History Review*.

Anthony Seldon
Diaries

Anthony Seldon examines the uses and pitfalls of diaries as tools for historians.

Some years ago tremendous excitement was generated when historians, their names unknown to the public, appeared nightly on television offering their views and contradicting each other. The episode? It was alleged that Hitler's diaries had been found and were soon to be published. Historians fell over each other in excitement or anger but all agreed that, if they were genuine, they would constitute the greatest historical discovery of the century.

They were fakes. But the issue reminds us quite how important a source diaries can be. This article will examine who writes diaries, and why, and their value and dangers to historians.

Who keeps diaries?

Many leading figures in the last 200 years have written diaries – politicians, military commanders, scientists, artists and others. Even civil servants, normally perceived to be retiring figures, have written diaries. Indeed, probably the most famous diarist of all, Samuel Pepys, was a civil servant, who worked in the Admiralty in the seventeenth century.

Until the general spread of literacy within the last hundred years, diaries tended to be written by the 'élites' in society, not only those who could write, but also those who possessed paper, and the space in the day to be able to write down their thoughts. Since then there have been larger numbers of diaries kept by the great majority of British people who never achieve eminence, and some are of great interest to historians, recording for example the experience of life during the interwar depression, or during the blitz in the Second World War.

The diaries of greatest interest to historians, however, remain those written by the eminent and powerful, or by those close to them. The eleventh volume of Gladstone's diary, covering just three years and taking up 708 printed pages, was recently published. This provides an extraordinary insight, not just into the mind of one of the most powerful Prime Ministers of the last century, but also of the broader political world.

No political diary in the twentieth century can match it. The long-serving Prime Ministers, Lloyd George, Baldwin, Churchill, Attlee and

Wilson kept no comparable personal record, nor apparently has Thatcher. Macmillan (Prime Minister 1957–63) did keep a full diary, which formed the basis of his six-volume memoirs, but in the main the most interesting political diaries have been published by those who never rose to the top office, including cabinet ministers like Leo Amery, Hugh Dalton and Barbara Castle, or by those who worked closely with the powerful, like John Colville and Harold Nicolson. The recordings of those who at close hand observe history being made can often be more illuminating than the jottings of the decision-takers themselves.

Diary-keeping has probably declined since the mid-twentieth century, largely due to great demand on politicians' time. The tape-recorder has been a valuable device for the diarist since the 1960s, with Tony Benn, the most prolific diary-keeper since the war, adopting the now common practice of speaking the diary onto a tape, to be subsequently typed up. Overall, diary-keeping may probably have declined, but caution is required: we do not know whether large numbers of diaries have been kept in secret, to be sprung on the world at a later date.

Motives for diary-keeping

The question of why diaries are written is not just one of idle interest. For the historian to assess the value and accuracy of a diary, or indeed of any source, he must consider why the document came into existence. The main motives for diary-keeping would appear to be: record-keeping and as an aide-mémoire; the psychological need to justify one's own actions and vent frustrations; an almost disinterested desire to preserve contemporary observations for the historical record; self-aggrandisement and a desire to make money, probably through securing publication. These motives are not discrete: commonly at least two or more are operative.

To understand motive is, therefore, *de rigueur* for the historian: hope of eventual publication, and settlement of old scores (a forlorn expectation) does not invalidate a diary, but they might well make the historian more critical when evaluating its content and value as a source. The desire to preserve thoughts for the historical record is laudable, and might well imply a balanced diary, mercifully free of bias. But might not the writer distort the importance of the events described, or people discussed, to make the content appear more noteworthy?

Value

This thought brings us to the third aspect of diary-keeping: their value to the historian. Every historical source, from newspaper cuttings to records of Cabinet meetings, can yield important material for the historian, but diaries can be more valuable than any. Why? Part of the reason lies in the length of time over which diaries are written: one can have a consistent thread running over perhaps 30 or 40 years of history, and the individual foibles of the diarist can be known and taken into account by the historian. The diarist provides personal feelings and comments where minutes of meetings (e.g. of the British Cabinet, which only have been kept since 1916) can be impersonal and often bland, when they exist at all. The diaries of Tony Benn, Barbara Castle and Richard Crossman are likely to remain invaluable complements to the Cabinet records of the 1964–70 Labour government even after they become fully available in 2001. Diaries can provide atmosphere and colour which give the reader a better sense of the events and personalities described. Chips Channon's accounts of High Life in London Society in the 1930s, for example, are vivid and often scintillating, and very much convey a sense of what it must have been like to be there at the time. Diaries can also provide a mass of information and detail which might otherwise have been lost, filling gaps where there is no satisfactory alternative source. The diary of Hugh Gaitskell (who was leader of the Labour Party 1955–63) is full of such material.

Dangers

But diaries can also, like any other source, mislead and distort. How much credence should one give them? It is often difficult to evaluate. Diaries can exaggerate the importance of the writer's own standing and influence (conveying a misleading impression of their author's centrality to the events described). Diaries written up daily and which describe very recent developments can suffer from an excess of passion: Alan Brooke (the senior military chief for most of the Second World War) frequently exploded in his diary about the impossible Winston Churchill. This can give the historian an overly jaundiced view of their relationship. Yet diaries written up only at the weekend, or at longer intervals are obviously at a greater distance from the events they describe. These can smooth over the true feelings of the heat of the moment, and confuse the sequence of events.

Diaries, it should be remembered, are just one person's record, often jotted down in haste, of feelings at a particular point in time. At worst, they are dull, plodding and misleading; at best, as with Adrian Mole's, witty, colourful, and full of insight.

Anthony Seldon's latest book is *The Major Effect*, co-edited with Dennis Kavanagh. He is also the editor (with Stuart Ball) of *The Conservative Century*.

Peter Catterall
Autobiographies and Memoirs

Autobiographies might seem to be ideal historical sources as 'eyewitness accounts.' However, their value must not be take for granted.

History is the record of human progress, achievements and endeavour. A particular view of it might be that it is the sum of the myriad individual histories that have helped to shape its course. It was perhaps in this sense that Ralph Waldo Emerson argued 'There is properly no history – only biography'. Published memoirs trace some at least of the individual histories of those who have in some way participated in or observed the course of history.

The records of individual lives, however eminent, will not of course provide a comprehensive record of the times through which they lived, although some of the more ambitious autobiographies certainly attempt to place the life recounted within a broader historical context. Nor can they obviate the need to consult other forms of evidence, even when studying events in which their subjects were intimately involved. They can of course cast considerable light on these events both in the form of additional evidence and through providing a personal insight into a particular matter. For instance, the memoirs of Walter Citrine,[1] the then General Secretary of the TUC, and of Ben Turner,[2] a member of the General Council, are of considerable value in reconstructing the TUC's handling of the 1926 General Strike and attempting to understand its reasons for eventually ending it. They however cannot place in historical context or provide a comprehensive picture of either the Strike itself, which involved thousands of workers and emergency measures by the government including the deployment of troops, nor of the actions of the General Council, except in so far as to explain why and how they themselves acted as they did.

The value of personal insight

In doing so they do manage to convey the sense of frustration with the miners' leaders and their lack of control and information which helped to doom the Strike. However, not all autobiographies succeed in recapturing the flavour of the moment. It is more contemporaneous sources such as diaries, letters and minutes that are written with partial knowledge of the course of events and their outcome. Autobiographies give a more complete and rounded picture, but it is not always one which accurately reflects what and why the subject felt and acted as he did at the time. Instead they necessarily impose some structure on the story and on the often inchoate processes of personal development. This can however be of considerable value in providing a rationalisation of the subject's attitudes and personal response to the social and cultural dilemmas of the period. Thus, Beatrice Webb's first volume of autobiography[3] deals extensively with her religious crises and doubts. This is a facet of many of the autobiographies of the period and provides useful evidence of the character of the religious uncertainty of the late Victorian era. Autobiography thus can contribute greatly to an understanding of cultural history. It can also contribute to an understanding of specific developments. Valuable insights into movements such as Chartism or the early history of the Labour Party can be gained from the autobiographies of people such as Thomas Cooper[4] or Philip Snowden.[5]

Autobiography can also help to explain intent and motive. It was, for instance, only with the publication of Heinrich Brüning's memoirs in 1970[6] that it became clear that his period as Chancellor of Germany in the fateful years 1930–2 was not spent so much on trying to solve the economic problems facing his country as in deliberately exacerbating them in pursuit of particular political goals. An insight into intent and motive is particularly valuable when seeking to understand why long-settled political issues such as the Corn Laws or parliamentary reform were so hotly disputed at the time and the arguments that were advanced to support and oppose them. At the very least it can be used to supplement the more contemporary evidence of newspapers and parliamentary debates. It could also be argued that personal sources, such as autobiography, diaries and letters are of greater importance for earlier periods because the quality of other sources is less. They are, for instance, a mainstay of students of nineteenth-century British Cabinet government simply because Cabinet minutes were not kept before the twentieth century. Much of British party history also relies on memoirs and this remains true even when all the party archives, diaries and private papers have become available.

Autobiography can also provide an insight to the living and working conditions of the nineteenth-century working class as well as into the workings of nineteenth-century Cabinet. Certainly other sources, such as Royal Commission reports, official statistics and, by the end of the century, social surveys, should also be used. But though these analyse the condition of the poor, few actually convey the experience of the workhouse, of unemployment or of the miner's cottage.

Motives and drawbacks

Not all autobiographies however are terribly revealing. Even Denis Healey's recent volume,[7] much praised though it was for its literary quality, does not greatly advance our knowledge of his work or of the governments in which he served. Many early Labour autobiographies, though strong on anecdotes, are short on contents. Few autobiographies however become, like David Niven's,[8] a vehicle for amusing anecdotes, not all of which occurred strictly as reported. Niven, as his biographer comments, did not 'necessarily regard the purpose of his autobiographies as being to tell the true story of his own life';[9] nor do they reveal much of the man, a facet of other autobiographies by celebrated actors such as Laurence Olivier.

Sheridan Morley's comments on Niven should remind readers of autobiographies as historical evidence of the importance of checking the motives of the author. Many autobiographies may be the result of a career break enforced by illness, loss of office or old age. This does not mean that they are purely the product of mellow reflection from which the grinding of axes is entirely absent. Lloyd George's *War Memoirs* for instance, although written as the result of illness, are, as his preface makes clear, a contribution to the debate over the conduct of the First World War, which other autobiographers had already entered, designed in part to arraign, in the words of the foreword to the 1938 edition

> the incompetence of the trained inexperts ... in the ghastly butchery of a series of vain and insane offensives.[10]

Lloyd George's response to the criticisms of him from generals such as Sir Frederick Maurice, has helped to ensure a continuing historiographical debate over military strategy in the Great War. The nature and origins of this debate bears out the validity of Jeremy Moon's caveat:

> It must, of course, be borne in mind that memoirs provide a useful method of retrospective justification for policies made and stands taken.[11]

In the process autobiographers may exaggerate their own role in events, may report as fact what is only hearsay or, as the result of the vagaries of memory, distort the sequence of events. The recollection of personal relationships is also likely to be distorted. As Snowden put it: the autobiographer 'must write of persons with whom he has been in intimate relationship. He cannot be quite frank in his estimate of them unless his honest opinion is wholly favourable'.[12]

Readers of autobiographies as historical sources should also ascertain the sources on which they were based. The major reason why Harold Macmillan and Hugh Dalton wrote amongst the most historical and detailed of twentieth-century political autobiographies is because they had their own copious diaries on which to base their narrative. Lloyd George did not keep a diary but had his own volumi-nous collection of papers. Edwin Plowden had a research assistant to refresh his memory with material from the Public Record Office.[13] Some autobiographies are indeed more or less ghosted for their 'author' by a research assistant. This is not without its dangers. As John Barnes points out, the research assistant may 'establish a frame-work of fact that owes little to the author's memory, and which could prompt the author to mend his own recollection ... In this way myths can be perpetuated for years.'[14]

Memoirs by ministers written relatively close to the events described may rely on privileged access to public records which other-wise remain closed. This supplies the detail, to which they are able to add their recollections of personalities and flesh out their own motives and the interplay of argument behind the development of particular policies. Obviously the closer to the events being described that this is written and the less it depends solely on the author's memory (Plowden for instance checked details with a great many contempo-raries) the more reliable it is likely to be. This consideration is of partic-ular importance when using the autobiographies of élite figures. Doubts about the reliability of the detail in the relevant autobiogra-phies and the relative wealth of documentary sources may explain the reluctance of diplomatic historians to make much use of the former. This concern is generally less for social or economic historians absorbed less with the minutiae of policy-making than with attitudes, impressions, behaviour and usage. Meanwhile, for art historians, autobiography can be vital in tracing artistic development and the responses of writers, painters and musicians to their cultural milieu.

Not all autobiographical writing is autobiography. Although the distinction between autobiography and memoir has been eroded in recent years, the former is strictly speaking the story of a life whilst the latter records a particular event, institution or movement from the author's standpoint and through the author's part in it.

The value of autobiography and memoirs has not been universally appreciated. 'All history is gossip and the least reliable of all is history in the form of biography or autobiography' was Aneurin Bevan's dis-missive comment.[15] Certainly many autobiographies do not rise far above the level of chatty reminiscences. Others, however, provide a personal history of institutions or events which is of great value as a historical source and as a way of understanding not only those events and institutions but the individuals who helped to shape them. History without the insights of personality that these help to bring is not only dry, but unbalanced.

Notes

(1) Citrine, Walter *Men and Work* (Hutchinson, 1964).
(2) Turner, Ben *About Myself* (Cayme Press, 1930).
(3) Webb, Beatrice *My Apprenticeship* (Longmans Green and Co., 1926).
(4) Cooper, Thomas *The Life of Thomas Cooper* (Hodder and Stoughton, 1872).
(5) Snowden, Philip *Autobiography* (2 vol.) (Nicolson and Watson, 1934).
(6) Brüning, Heinrich *Memoiren 1918–1934* (1970).
(7) Healey, Denis *The Time of My Life* (Michael Joseph, 1989).
(8) Niven, David *The Moon's a Balloon* (Hamilton, 1971); *Bring on the Empty Horses*, (Hamilton, 1975).
(9) Morley, Sheridan *David Niven: The Other Side of the Moon* (Weidenfeld and Nicolson, 1985).
(10) Lloyd George, David *War Memoirs I* (Odhams, 1938) pp. v-vi.
(11) Moon, Jeremy 'Post-War British political memoirs' *Parliamentary Affairs 35* (1982) p. 224.
(12) Snowden, pp. 6–7.
(13) Plowden, Edwin *An Industrialist in the Treasury* (Andre Deutsch, (1989) p. xiii.
(14) Barnes, John 'Books and Journals' in Anthony Seldon (ed.) *Contemporary History: Practice and Method* (Blackwell, 1988) p. 37.
(15) Jones, G. W. 'The value of recent biographies, autobiographies and diaries', *Parliamentary Affairs 34* (1981) p. 335.

Peter Catterall is the Director of the Institute of Contemporary British History, Visiting Lecturer in History at Queen Mary and Westfield College, London and editor of the *Modern History Review*.

Malcolm Barr-Hamilton
Local Records

Archives in local record offices can supply rich sources for the study not only of local history but also of social history and of the local dimensions of national organisations, such as political parties and trade unions.

Records or archives are created as the result of an administrative or legal process or transaction by an individual or organisation. Many such documents, no longer generally required for administrative purposes, but which are considered important historically, are placed in record or archive offices where members of the public can examine them. Material held in record offices represents a rich source for the study of local history.

There are over 160 local record offices in the British Isles. All the English and Welsh county councils operate centrally-placed record offices and some also have local branch offices serving particular areas of a county. In Scotland each of the regions operate record offices. In addition many district and borough councils operate archive services, sometimes combined with local history libraries. There are a number of directories available listing local record offices.

The content of local record offices does, of course, vary not inconsiderably from one to another; however there are certain general types of record that are common to most record offices. This article will examine some of the most widely found and used of such records.

Not surprisingly, often the greater part of material held in local record offices is made up of the records of the local authorities themselves and their predecessors. As a result of considerable parliamentary legislation in the Victorian period many new types of local authorities were introduced to deal with specific problems, in addition to long-standing bodies such as borough corporations and parish vestries. Such new local authorities included Boards of Guardians of the Poor (also known as Poor Law Boards) to deal with the growing problem of poverty, Highway Boards to deal with roads, Local Boards of Health and Rural Sanitary Authorities to tackle the great and related problems of sanitation and health. The modern system of multi-functional local government can be traced back to the end of the nineteenth century with the introduction of county councils in 1888 and urban and rural district councils in 1894.

By far the commonest type of records to survive of local authorities are the minutes of the board or council or of its committees and sub-committees. These record the decisions take at meetings. Typically for the nineteenth century they take the form of large hand-written volumes subsequently becoming typewritten or printed. They are a most important source for numerous subject areas such as sanitation, the provision of street lighting, council houses, local public transport, hospitals and education.

Minutes of meetings vary enormously from one authority to another and for the same authority at different periods. Some are very detailed giving, apparently, a full transcript of the discussions that took place, while others can be frustatingly brief and in the extreme being merely a list of decisions taken with, for example, no indication of the extent of opposition to a motion. Where they survive, agenda papers can be of more use to the historian than the minutes themselves. These may include detailed reports on various subjects by officers of the council.

Rate books

Rate books are a type of record which often, but not always, survives in large quantities. The system of local rating has its origins in the sixteenth century. A property-based tax, the rating system involved regularly assessing the value of property, the assessments being entered into rate books. Typically a nineteenth-century rate book will have a brief description of the location and nature of the property (cottage and garden, etc), the name of the owner and occupier together with the extent of the property, its rateable value and the amount of rate payable. They are therefore invaluable for the study of such things as the ownership and occupancy of the property or urban growth. They are not, however, the easiest of sources to use. Properties are not usually listed alphabetically by street or owner but in a sort of geographical sequence and seldom are they indexed. In the nineteenth century, before the general advent of street numbering, it can take time and patience to identify particular properties. Also it is not always clear if the owners and occupiers shown are the actual owners and occupiers or lessees and sub-tenants.

Correspondence of the clerk to the council or board or of other officers such as the surveyor or engineer can sometimes reveal more than can be found in minute books. In the nineteenth century, correspondence was usually written into general letterbooks, though often these were indexed. In the twentieth century the correspondence file has emerged, more often than not one file conveniently dealing with each subject.

An important and graphic source for the study of buildings and businesses are plans submitted to local authorities in accordance with sanitary, building and town planning regulations. Many of these in recent years have been transferred to record offices while others remain largely inaccessible to the public, in council planning departments. Included with the applications are detailed plans of buildings showing, for example, the internal arrangements of houses, or of whole housing estates showing such things as the density of housing and provision of public amenities. As with any original source care must be taken when using these: applications will generally include those not approved by the council as well as those approved. The existence of plans of building approved by the council does not necessarily mean that the building was ever actually built.

Parish records

The records of many (but by no means all) Anglican parishes can be found in local record offices. These will include registers of baptisms, marriages and burials. For the modern period these are not the vital source for population studies that they are for earlier periods, as civil registration of births, marriages and deaths was introduced in 1837. However, they can be used to shed light on such things as social structure, occupations and literacy. Other records often found are the minutes of the vestry and from 1926, the parochial church council and its committees. These can be a very useful source for the study of church restoration and rebuilding in Victorian times. Students of theology may find lively debate of such matters in these minutes. Registers of church services where surviving give a good indication of how high or low a church was in the Anglican spectrum. Records of church schools such as log books (the head teacher's diary recording details of attendance, staffing and discipline, etc), admission registers and the minutes of meetings of school managers are sometimes to be found among parish records.

A most important historical source often located among parish records are tithe maps and awards. Following the Tithe Commutation Act of 1836 detailed parish maps were produced together with schedules indicating the owners and occupiers of property and its state of cultivation. This makes an excellent starting point for the study of a locality in Victorian times.

The records of some non-conformist churches have been deposited. As with Anglican records these might include registers of baptisms or members, marriages (if the church was licensed for this purpose) and burials (if the church had a burial ground). Clearly these are important for studying the development of non-conformity in a locality and for identifying the religious persuasions of persons prominent in local businesses or politics. Minutes of meetings of church leaders are not uncommon.

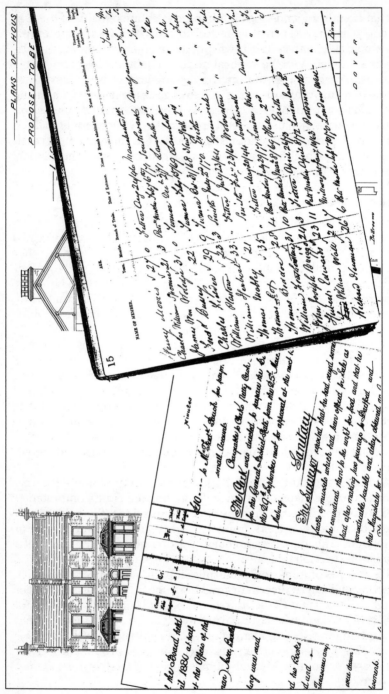

Some examples of the many local records available to the interested reader.

The records of some local clubs, societies and institutions have found their way into local record offices, though these represent a small proportion of the total of such bodies. These might range from sports clubs, debating societies, youth organisations, to political organisations and trade union branches. Typically such records will include minutes of the meetings of the committee running the organisation, and perhaps the secretary's correspondence and the treasurer's account books. Registers of members can be particularly useful, for example, for establishing the powerbase of a local political party or ratepayers' association. The admissions register of a local trade union branch may give information about the member's last employment and place of origin thus providing, for example, data on the pattern of migration of workers to a newly-developing industrial area.

Some record offices have very extensive holdings of business records of local firms ranging from small shopkeepers to large industrial concerns. Such records tend to be miscellaneous in nature but may include minute books recording meetings of directors and shareholders. These are most useful for the period before 1870, after which they tend to be rather formal. Correspondence and account books can reveal a wealth of information about the activities of a business, its customers, shareholders and workforce.

Private papers

Family and personal papers and private estate records often comprise a large proportion of a record office's holdings, ranging from individual letters and documents to very extensive archives. Correspondence and diaries can be a rich source for social history. Needless to say such documentation mainly relates to upper and middle-class society. Diaries of working-class people are rare, or at least rarely find their way into record offices.

The records of landed estates can be put to various uses. Title deeds (documenting the transfer of ownership or of the leasing of property) can be used to study the development of large estates or their subsequent break-up. These are, however, not easy to use because of the legal jargon involved. Account books and correspondence, if surviving, can make a useful source for the study of farming or industrial enterprises. Estate maps graphically show the extent of properties owned and to whom they were leased.

Census returns

Many record offices actively collect copies of local material held elsewhere such as the archives of central government at the Public Record Office in London, either as photocopies or in microform. Most commonly held are the census enumerator's returns for the 1841, 1851,

1861, 1871, 1881 and 1891 censuses. These are arranged by parish and show the relationship of household members to the head of the household; the sex, age and marital status of all members of the household together with occupations and place of birth (though in the 1841 census the information is more limited). These returns are therefore a vital source for any local social history or population study for the second half of the nineteenth century. One must however be aware that there can be inaccuracies, particularly with regard to ages and places of birth, and the enumerator's handwriting sometimes presents considerable difficulty.

In order to appreciate their limitations it is important to keep in mind, when using old records, the purpose for which they were originally created, which was not as an aid to historical research!

Further Reading

Foster, J. and Sheppard, J. *British Archives: A Guide to Archive Resources in the United Kingdom* (Macmillan, 1989).

Richardson, J. *The Local Historian's Encyclopaedia* (Historical Publications, 1986).

Royal Commission on Historical Manuscripts, *Record Repositories in Great Britain: a geographical directory* (HMSO, 1991).

Stephens, W.B. *Sources for English Local History* (Cambridge University Press, 1981).

Malcolm Barr-Hamilton is archivist at the Bexley Local Studies Centre.

Edwin Green
Business Archives

All companies generate and keep archives. But what do these tell us of social and economic changes and conditions?

The archives of firms, companies and other business institutions are one of the richest but least well-known sources for the modern historian. The United Kingdom, with its exceptionally long industrial and business history, can claim to hold many of the largest series of business records in the world. Over the past 20 years these collections have been made available to a growing number and variety of historians from home and overseas.

This article describes how this unusual resource is of value to a wide range of historians. Certainly business archives have a special importance for economic historians in general and business historians in particular. Yet businesses reflect change in society as a whole and historians can now turn to business archives for a wealth of information about customers, shareholders, staff, products and property. Business archives in the United Kingdom are no longer the exclusive and private domain of the company historian.

Pedigree

Business archives in this country have a long and interesting pedigree. In the fourteenth century the London livery companies and gilds of Norwich and Bristol created long series of registers, mainly as a record of apprenticeship. By the seventeenth century goldsmith-bankers were accumulating large collections of records, partly to keep track of safe custody items but later as a record of banking transactions.

The development of business record-keeping, however, was mainly the work of joint-stock companies. Operating according to agreed rules of business, the joint-stock companies were responsible for keeping specific types of records and reporting back their performance to shareholders. Examples in the late seventeenth and early eighteenth centuries included the Bank of England and the Bank of Scotland, an insurance companies such as the Sun Fire Office and Royal Exchange. From the 1820s and 1830s this formal record-keeping became a feature of all types of joint-stock companies, mining and exploration concerns and the railway companies, as well as a new generation of banks and insurance companies. Other sectors of British business were not so affected by the rules of joint-stock legislation but nevertheless accumulated large collections of records for purely practical purposes. The extensive records of British brewers and distillers, for example, were retained both as a working guide to recipes and output and for tax and excise reasons. Manufacturers such as shipbuilders and locomotive engineers held on to the specifications and drawings of their products for the simple reason that customers would need replacement parts or repeat orders.

In this way, many of the country's outstanding collections were retained for business reasons or out of legal compulsion. A wider role for business archives did not emerge until the early years of this century. This was partly an awakening of interest in the industrial past (the Wedgwood Museum was opened as early as 1906) and partly the result of a new enthusiasm for publishing company histories. Between 1901 and 1940, for example, no less than 650 books and pamphlets on business and company history were published in this country.

The growth of interest in company history slowly encouraged the development of distinct archives departments within companies. The Bank of England established its Roehampton records office in the early years of the century and in 1933 J.A. Giuseppi was given special responsibility for the Bank's history and archives. Further development of in-house archives was delayed until after the Second World War, and even by the mid-1960s there were no more than a dozen full or part-time archivists in company posts. By comparison the growth in company archives in the last 25 years has been dramatic, with at least 100 and perhaps as many as 150 now employed specifically as company archivists.

At the same time many collections of business archives were finding their way into national or local record offices. In some cases companies deposited their records as an alternative to maintaining an in-house archive. In other cases record offices or museums acquired business archives by outright purchase or as a result of a liquidation or receivership. The rescue of the records of Upper Clyde Shipbuilders (now at the Scottish Record Office and the University of Glasgow), Handley-Page (at the Royal Air Force Museum) and Jensen Motors (at the Modern Records Centre, University of Warwick) are important examples. The development of these resources means that the modern historian has a wide choice of business collections, available either in private company archives or in public record offices. But what do these collections contain and how can the historian make use of them?

Records types and uses

The contents of business collections do not follow an exact formula. Like any other historical source, they reflect the structure of the parent organisation and the nature of their business activity. There is little in common, for example, between the records of an international motor manufacturer and the archives of a corner-shop retailer. Nevertheless most business collections have the following characteristics which give them direct value to the modern historian.

(a) Corporate records

The corporate records of a business include the partnership agreements (for firms) or deeds of settlement or articles of association (for joint-stock companies). These documents are more revealing than they might seem, as they are the legal statement of the objectives of the business and they provide lists of the original partners or shareholders. For companies established over the last 200 years, however, the most valuable source is the minute books of the board of directors. These records give details of the decisions of business – the big strategic decisions on launching a new product or acquiring another business, the routine decisions relating to staff and premises, and decisions affecting customers and suppliers. Directors' minutes over the past 50 years have become increasingly formal, but they remain the 'core' source for historians interested in the company *per se*. In complete contrast, corporate records such as shareholders' registers are an invaluable source for local historians and for historians of wealth and occupations. Share registers provide details of investors' addresses, occupational and family inheritance as well as purely financial information.

(b) Accounting records

Many historians (and archivists) are nervous or alarmed at the prospect of using the accounting records of firms and companies. The hierarchy of book-keeping – cash books, journals, private ledgers, general ledgers – is not user-friendly. Even so, these records offer an extraordinary range of evidence for business historians and for historians interested in particular trades, products and communities. In the age of the personal computer, some historians are discovering that these sources (when put into database form) are more manageable than they had expected. Researchers interested in the inner workings of a company can use accounting records to reconstruct its capital and profitability – information which is not always available in published reports and accounts. The ledgers and cash books can also be analysed to identify customers and suppliers of the firm or company. Conversely, fine art historians and biographers have used accounting records to identify patrons, buyers and dealers of works of art.

(c) Production records

The production records of a business vary greatly according the nature of the enterprise. In the manufacturing sector specification books and sales registers are of obvious value to industrial historians, enthusiasts and collectors. Similarly the production records of the extractive industries illustrate the vital role of coal, gas, oil and minerals in modern economic development. In many cases these records of production are supported by collections of photographs and technical drawings, marketing literature and advertisements. This combination of sources allows the historian to assess not only the products and manufacturing methods of the past, but also the changing markets for British goods.

In the non-manufacturing sector, the archives of banks, insurance companies, building societies, and transport and retail services all contain registers of their business. These registers, like production and sales records, are essentially a record of transactions between the supplier and the customer. This type of information is a richer source for the historian than it might appear. A classic example is the series of fire insurance policy registers produced by the great insurance companies from the 1690s onwards. These records (notably the Sun, Royal Exchange and Hand-in-Hand collections at the Guildhall Library) give details of the policyholder and his or her occupation, the insured property and contents and the insured value. These records have proved their worth for many different types of research, from major investigations into the industrial revolution to local studies of single streets or buildings. Most of the other service industries have produced parallel sets of business registers, in which the information about former customers is as useful – if not more so – as the evidence about the business itself. The great virtue of such collections is that they provide data about businesses, properties and individuals which otherwise have left little or no trace of their existence.

(d) Personnel records

Businesses, like any other modern organisation, also produce and retain personnel records. A company's registers of staff and salaries give vital statistics of employment patterns and working conditions locally and nationally. On a more specific level these records are a useful source for biographers and family historians, although access to confidential files is not always possible.

(e) Property and investment records

The property and investment records of businesses can also come to the aid of the historian, particularly if the researcher is interested in a particular building, site or street. Companies in the banking, brewing and retailing industries are major owners and occupants of property on the high streets of Britain. In recent years a growing number of local historians, civic societies and architectural historians have turned to these sources, which can also be useful for school history and geography projects. In this way property records, like the other major categories of business archives, have a value far beyond the special needs of company history. They are a large and a relatively unexploited resource of historians throughout the spectrum of the subject.

Locating business archives

The historian interested in using business archives has a wide choice of sources and locations.[1] For research on a particular company, the computerised 'business index' at the National Register of Archives (NRA) at the Royal Commission on Historical Manuscripts hugely simplifies the initial search. The index contains the names of over 23,000 companies or firms whose records are held in private and public record offices. The index also serves as a guide to the business archive lists accumulated by the NRA since its foundation in 1945.

Historians studying particular industries and professions can now turn to a number of published guides to business archives. The Royal Commission on Historical Manuscripts has produced a guide to the records of the textile and leather sector between 1760 and 1914 and a further volume on engineering appeared in 1994.[2] The Business Archives Council, which was formed in 1934 to encourage the preservation of business archives, has also published a number of guides to the archives of sectors of industry. Its current series, *Studies in British Business Archives,* already includes detailed guides to the archives of brewing and shipbuilding.[3] A guide to the records of chartered accountants in England and Wales (in association with the Institute of Chartered Accountants) has been published, and the council is also preparing a new survey of the archives of British banking.

In contrast to these sectoral guides, the Business Archives Council has also produced a guide to the records of the oldest registered companies in England and Wales.[4] This guide, *Company Archives,* includes the results of a major survey carried out between 1980 and 1984; it lists the records of over 650 companies registered between 1856 and 1889, together with archive lists of another 1,000 associated companies. The unusual feature of the guide is the range of business enterprises covered by the survey – not only basic manufacturing and service industries but also trading and property companies and companies established specifically for sports or entertainment. The guide is yet another reminder of the breadth of interest which business archives offer to the history community.

The position of business archives in this country is not static, however, and historians using these sources should watch out for new arrivals in local record offices. Each year the Royal Commission on Historical Manuscripts publishes *Accessions to Repositories and Reports Added to the National Register of Archives*. Specific references to business archives in *Accessions to Repositories* are abstracted for publication in *Business Archives: Sources and History*, the journal of the Business Archives Council. New arrivals in Scottish record offices, together with news of recent surveys of business records, are reported in *Scottish Industrial History*, the journal of the Business Archives Council of Scotland.

Access to business archives

Researchers wishing to consult business archives held in public or local record offices will find that the conditions of access are similar to those for other types of archives. Because business archives are often very bulky, however, some record offices hold these records off-site and may need additional notice of a visit. In some cases the companies or families who deposited the records may have requested the closure of records of recent date. In most cases that limit is 30 or 50 years, but exceptionally owners have specified a limit of as much as 100 years. Certain depositors also require record offices to notify them of any substantial research proposals affecting their records.

The arrangements for access to in-house company archives vary greatly. Details of over 70 major collections in this country , including conditions of access, are provided in the *Directory of Corporate Archives*, published by the Business Archives Council.[5] Nevertheless a number of common factors have emerged in recent years. Most company archives do not have the staffing or resources of a local record office, so that researchers should give ample notice of a visit. Some companies also ask for the name of, or a reference from, the supervisor of the research and may ask the researcher to allow the company to see any text based on its records before publication. Certain sensitive categories of records – for example, individual personnel files or records relating the third parties – may not be available for research. However, as long as the researcher is aware beforehand that there may be restrictions, these hurdles should not be a discouragement. If a company has taken the trouble and expense to establish an archives unit, then the researcher can generally expect a helpful response and can look forward to using some of the most valuable but least exploited types of historical source.

Notes

(1) See also Orbell, J. *A Guide to Tracing the History of a Business* (Business Archives Council, 1987).

(2) Royal Commission on Historical Manuscripts *Records of Business and Industry 1760–1914: Textiles and Leather* (HMSO, 1990). *Records of Business and Industry 1760–1914: Metal-processing and Engineering* (HMSO, 1994).

(3) Richmond, L. and Turton, A. *The Brewing Industry: A Guide to Historical Records* (Manchester University Press, 1990); Ritchie, A. *The Shipbuilding Industry: A Guide to Historical Records* (Manchester University Press, 1992).

(4) Richmond, L. and Stockford, B. *Company Archives: The Survey of the Records of 1000 of the First Registered Companies in England and Wales* (Gower, 1986).

(5) Richmond, L. and Turton, A. *Directory of Corporate Archives* (Business Archives Council, 3rd edn 1992).

Edwin Green is Archivist of Midland Bank plc and a Visiting Fellow at the City University.

Glenn R. Wilkinson
Newspapers

Newspapers are both a source of information for the historian and a major influence on the history of their times. It is therefore important for the student of history to understand the nature of this source and its historical significance.

Newspapers offer historians a unique approach to the study of the past but, as with all source materials, they need to be handled with caution and a critical eye. Studies of the press and journalism have in the past tended to concentrate on personalities; the owners, editors and journalists involved in the production process. Other historians, such as political, diplomatic and military historians, have used newspapers as a peripheral source to augment arguments raised by other sources. While these approaches are valuable in themselves, they tend to neglect the treasure-trove of information contained within the pages of newspapers. Increasing interest in social history, however, has resulted in the development of new approaches to newspapers as a source, such as examining the process of production, the role of editors and journalists, patterns of ownership and so on. More specifically, an analysis of the content in newspapers can tell us quite a lot about the society of which they were a part; interests, lifestyle patterns, leisure activities, and perspectives on the world. In looking at the newspapers in such an original way, historians have had to find new theories of how to think about this source and come up with the new methods of how to use it. To do this, it is necessary to evaluate the advantages of newspapers over the 'reflection–manipulation' debate, and have a fresh look at the different parts of the paper and what they reveal.

Value of newspapers

Newspapers are a particularly valuable source because of the very nature of their existence. Firstly, newspapers are, for the most part, regularly published at set intervals. This means that, unlike diaries and letters for example, there are no important pieces of the historical puzzle missing. Newspapers are also datable, so that the exact date, and even in some cases time, can be established, enabling historians to formulate a chronology of events and cultural changes, to locate data in time with pin-point accuracy, and to cross-reference their findings with other newspapers.

In addition, newspapers are time-specific and do not have an eye for posterity. They are designed to be read and passed on or discarded before the publication of the next issue, meaning that there is little question of concern for future reputations, as there could be with personal or public papers. Linked with this idea is the necessity for papers to find a contemporary audience in order to maintain circulation and stay in business. While great literature can be 'discovered' as such years after publication, newspapers must speak to a constituency immediately, and either react to their changing perspectives or, at least, relate news in ways which do not offend or contradict preconceived world views. Similarly, the specialised press can point to clues which help to illuminate such activities and interests as finance, leisure, trades and gender/age specific issues. These characteristics found in newspapers can act as the backbone of research for social or cultural historians or reinforce more traditional works.

Reflection versus manipulation

One of the major ongoing debates revolves around the question of whether newspapers 'reflect' the attitudes and perceptions of readers or whether readers are manipulated by the press into seeing the world in certain ways. Some historians believe that the press acts as a 'mirror' or 'barometer' to the society of which they are a part, reflecting currently dominant themes and showing the actual tastes of readers. This theory plays upon the idea that papers have no life outside their contemporary culturally-defined environment. Yet critics feel this approach is too simplistic. Historians must take into account the many layers or filters through which newspaper content must pass in the production process; the gathering of selected information, the editing and the presentation of news is extremely complex, as people buy papers for particular reasons; sports results, fashion pages, the serials, a crisis in the world or at home, as a political/ideological statement, or merely out of habit. They may not read the whole paper or agree with all its content all of the time, a problem if we are to assume readers are represented by press content. The difficult question of circulation and readership also contributes to the difficulties in assuming the press is a reflection of society, particularly before the days of accountable figures.

Critics of the 'reflection' school would argue that the press manipulates and influences readers to think and act in certain ways. Direct means of manipulation are those opinions and observations which are overtly stated, and are included most obviously in the editorial and feature articles. Indirect means of influence are conveyed in the way news is presented. Emphasis can be placed on certain stories and issues by merely placing them in key areas, such as on the front page or opposite the leader page. Typeface, headlines, space per story and the editing of photographs and captions are also indications of importance afforded to particular topics. Consideration must also be given to the fact that by the end of the nineteenth century, newspapers required large amounts of capital to start and maintain. This meant that the control of the medium was increasingly in the hands of upper and middle-class males, who either consciously or unconsciously filled their papers with their particular world view.

While these problems seem difficult to overcome, there are various techniques which can be used by historians to counteract the problem of manipulation. Firstly, researchers could 'cast their net' as widely as possible by looking at a variety of newspapers representing diverse perspectives such as ideology, target audience (class, gender and interest), publication frequency, cover price, geographical distribution and cross-ownership. Through this technique, the intentional and unintentional biases of individual papers can be avoided. A second technique involves understanding the social context of the period under examination. In order to claim manipulation existed, researchers must establish that there were reasons for manipulation, whether appropriate means existed and how issues were presented in other contexts. Also, readership patterns of the age must be understood to indicate whether people took more than one paper, whether they could easily change to another if they did not agree with their own, and the existence of other forms of media with which to compare the press. If readers could not change the source of their information or compare it with others, any attempts at manipulation either had to be extremely subtle or benefit from the acquiescence of readers, and play on their pre-conceived ideas. A third consideration involves an awareness of a point made earlier that as readers do not necessarily read all sections in the newspaper, the reception of a particular message will be incomplete. Further, the attentions to typeface, layout, headlines, etc. could simply be seen as sensitivity to reader interest and demand; knowing what topics sell newspapers and how they should be presented to emphasise them.

Content of the press

With these views in mind, the vast amount of information found in the pages of the press can be examined. The following represents only a few of the areas contained within newspapers which could be of use. The first and most obvious of these areas is the written images used to convey news and ideas to readers. These images are expressed in ways which are acceptable and understood by people who buy newspapers. An analysis of the way these images are made can tell us something about how people perceived particular events and issues. Illustrations and photographs offer similar insights into how people saw their world. The subjects chosen, the 'mood' created by the artist, what is emphasised or played down, the position and size of the visual element and the captions and surrounding text are just a few things which can be informative. Similarly, the images which accompany advertisements can indicate themes and perceptions which are 'saleable' to a potential consumer. Advertisers are very sensitive to public perception, as an image which offended or did not strike an audience as relevant to them would result in poor sales or an unfavourable product association and be changed quickly. In addition, advertisements can reveal fashions, lifestyles, the cost of living, working conditions and so on. Cartoons are also features where powerful yet simple images are conveyed, because cartoonists had to capture the sentiments or perceptions of readers in one simple drawing, which indicate that the images repeated over time were acceptable, familiar and understood. Other sections in the paper can tell historians intricate details of daily life such as what entertainments were popular with different classes and genders, how sporting events featured, audience reaction to speeches, concerts and films, relations between the sexes, the images in popular serialised stories and the issue of the day as expressed in letters to the editor.

These sections show that newspapers are an almost endless source of information for historians and can be valuable if used carefully. Probably the biggest problem with newspapers is the overwhelming amount of material they contain; the thousands of titles producing countless pages of information on a regular daily or weekly basis over the course of centuries. But this should not be seen as a daunting task – given specific limits, even the acres of newsprint can be accessible and rewarding for the intrepid historical adventurer.

Further Reading

Boyce, G. et al. (eds) *Newspaper History from the Seventeenth Century to the Present Day* (Constable Press 1978).
Brake, L. et al. (eds) *Investigating Victorian Journalism* (Macmillan, 1990).
Brown, L. *Victorian News and Newspapers* (Clarendon Press, 1985).
Koss, S. *The Rise and Fall of the Political Press in Britain*, Vols I and II (Hamish Hamilton, 1981).
Williams, F. *Dangerous Estates: The Anatomy of Newspapers* (Patrick Stevens 1957/1984).

Glenn R. Wilkinson is a postgraduate student at the University of Lancaster.

C. J. Morris
Film and Newsreel

The value of film as a historical source for twentieth-century history is that it not merely 'illustrates' the past, but has an influential role in the formation of public opinion.

Until recently, the potential value of studying film as a historical source of the twentieth century, be it newsreel, documentary, feature film or television, has been underestimated or regarded with scepticism by the majority of historians. When film has been employed by historians, it has often been used in an illustrative manner, not as a source which can assist in the interpretation of twentieth-century events. Film has largely been treated as entertainment or as an art form. Its description and examination has been limited to appreciation and assessment, much in the same way as one would evaluate a painting or sculpture. Analysis has focused upon the semiotic study of film, a study involving signs and symbols, or the study of the film's message structure. Film has been criticised as being shallow in depicting only the external appearance of events, rarely going beyond the descriptive and 'offering few insights into the processes and relationship, cause, and motives which are the historian's concern'.[1]

Film is a man-made medium. It can be unreliable, even faked, and it is edited to tell a particular 'story'. Essentially 'the art of cinema is the creation of illusion'.[2] Therefore, film should not be regarded as an objective record of past events: 'the film as a whole is not a remnant of the depicted sequence of events, but merely the film makers' reconstruction/model/account of it.'[3] The finished product results from the editing process after the event has taken place. The audience does not see the film in its original form, footage is discarded, there may be jumps in time and space, and authentic footage can be combined with the unreal or stock shots. The soundtrack can be dubbed later, music can be added for inspirational or emotive effect, and a 'seemingly factual' commentary can be added. All this, together with technical decisions made about camera lenses, distances, angles, etc, can distort the 'reality' which is supposedly being portrayed. The camera often lies!

Film can also influence the 'history' it is recording. The mere presence of a camera and awareness of its presence by those being filmed may even affect the course of events and its presentation. For example, many feared that the introduction of cameras in the House of

Commons would affect the quality of debate, with parliament becoming a media circus. Moreover, film is the product of a collaboration between many individuals and their interests. Producers, directors, cameramen, editors and writers all have some influence, which may be hard to quantify over the finished product. Hidden factors external to the film-making process, such as censorship by the British Board of Film Classification, the economic constraints of sponsorship, or studio politics, also influence the final form.

However, many of the criticisms of film as historical evidence, including the claim that it is 'partial, subjective, tendentious, emotive and even forged', can also be made against written and oral evidence.[4] Moreover, film evidence, like its written and oral counterparts, can be substantiated through other records, including the archives of studios, cameramen's reports, distributors' catalogues, memoirs, and official government documents, such as the British Board of Film Censors' script files housed in the British Film Institute.[5]

Historians have never relied upon a single source for their interpretation of history. It is noteworthy that criticisms of twentieth-century historians who use film as evidence have not been made against archaeologists who have sometimes had to 'rely entirely on visual evidence', such as cave paintings and Roman pots.[6] The value of film as a historical source which helps wider understanding of the twentieth century depends upon the questions the historian answers through its study. If the historian views film as evidence of what happened on a particular occasion, little can be added to the record beyond the descriptive, such as the surroundings, buildings, fashions, and voices of individuals. However, if the historian asks what the public was told about a particular event at the time, film takes on primary importance. The key to the examination of film as a historical source is the intention of the film maker and the message he wishes to propagate.

The twentieth-century communications revolution, the development of film as the first universal 'mass' medium to propagate information, and the use of film to persuade the public in a direct and immediate way demands the attention of the historian. The implications of mass attendances at the cinema and, later, mass viewing of television have not been lost on politicians, setting the twentieth century apart from previous epochs of history. In the 1930s, 40% of the British population went to the cinema at least once a week, and 25% attended twice a week or more.[7] Between 1945 and 1950, before television assumed primacy as a mass medium, 32% of adults still visited the cinema once a week, 13% attended more than once a week, and only 24% did not go at all.[8] Most who attended were young and working class. Politically this was significant because, with the advent of universal suffrage, developments in working-class movements, trade unionism, and conscription coincided with the development of film as a mass medium.

Moreover, unlike the growth of the press in the nineteenth century, the impact of film upon the working class was even greater because it demanded no literacy or education on the part of its audience. The possession of information, on which the decision-making process was based, was no longer the prerogative of the literate and educated ruling classes. Politicians and leaders from Chamberlain to Hitler and Stalin, democratic and totalitarian alike, recognised the implications of the communications revolution and film in particular as an instrument for political propaganda. Film can be seen in a number of ways, aesthetically as examination of itself and as part of the evolution of the film industry, as a product of a nation's culture, and as a medium for propaganda. However, film's greatest value to the historian may be its role in the formation of opinion.

> If the essence of political democracy is that it leaves political power, the responsibility for its use ultimately in the hands of the people, then communications and propaganda are a rather more essential part of the workings and therefore of the history of a democracy than a totalitarian state.[9]

In the democratic state, the element of coercion is missing, distinguishing the state's influence upon opinion from that of a totalitarian regime. In a democracy, the success and durability of the political system, as perceived by the government in power, depends upon the ability to persuade the mass not to oppose the system. For example, during the miners' strike in July 1984, Margaret Thatcher was the first serving Prime Minister to appear on a talk show, *Aspel and Company*, because she wanted to counter the portrayal of her by striking miners as a 'callous harpy'.[10] The memories of those who lived during World War Two often differ from the 'record', not because their perceptions were mistaken, but because their perceptions about the war they were fighting were moulded by the government.[11]

The influence of people's perceptions through the government's use and interpretation of film has continued to the present day. Therefore, it is not the impact of a single piece of film or a single film which is important but the cumulative effect of an audience's exposure to stereotypes and themes shaped by the ruling élite. Objections to film as an unreliable source of historical evidence can be overcome if one remembers that its value is that it records 'the media of public information in the century of the common man'.[12]

Notes

(1) Smith, P. (ed.) *The Historian and Film* (1976) p. 5.
(2) Grenville, J. A. S. *Film as History* (1971) p. 4.
(3) Fledelius, K. (1989) 'Audio-visual history: the development of a new field of research', *Historical Journal of Film, Radio and Television*, Vol. 9, No. 2, p. 156.
(4) Smith, p. 6.
(5) Short, K.R.M. (ed.) *Feature Film as History* (1981) p. 23.
(6) Grenville, p.6.
(7) Mowat, C.L. *Britain Between the Wars, 1918–40* (1966) p. 501.
(8) Marwick, A. *Britain in the Century of Total War* (1968) p. 360.
(9) Pronay, N. and Spring, D.W. *Propaganda, Politics, and Films, 1918–1945* (1982) p. 18.
(10) Cockerell, M. *Live from No. 10: The Inside Story of Prime Ministers and Television* (1988) pp. 228–9.
(11) Taylor, P. (ed.) *Britain and the Cinema in the Second World War* (1988) pp. 2–3.
(12) Pronay, N. 'The moving picture and historical research', *Journal of Contemporary History* Vol. 18, No. 3. (1983) p. 411.

Further Reading

Aldgate, A. *Cinema and History: British Newsreels and the Spanish Civil War.* (1979).
Curran, J. and Porter, V. (eds) *British Cinema History* (1983).
Dickenson, M. and Street, S. (eds) *Cinema and State: The Film Industry and British Government 1927–1984* (1985).
Oliver, E. (ed.) *Researchers 'Guide to British Film and Television Collections* (1980).
Pronay, N. 'British newsreels in the 1930s: Audience and producers', *History* (1971).
Pronay, N. 'British newsreels in the 1930s: Policies and impact', *History* (1972).
Robertson, J.C. *The British Board of Film Censors* (1985).
Sorlin, P. *The Film in History – Restaging the Past* (1980).

C. J. Morris is a doctoral student at the Institute for Communications Studies at the University of Leeds.

Colin Seymour-Ure and Liz Ottaway
Cartoons

Colin Seymour-Ure and Liz Ottaway assess the value of a particular, and rather slippery, kind of documentary evidence – cartoons.

Picture Hitler, and most of us will think of the toothbrush moustache, the forelock and perhaps the strutting gait. This is the classic image, and cartoonists such as David Low (1891–1963) have arguably fixed it more than anyone else in the minds of succeeding generations.

Such is the power of the cartoon. At its highest, as the art historian E. H. Gombrich put it, the cartoon 'solidifies the elusive flux of events into a manageable or memorable myth'. Cartoons of Hitler give us an instantly recognisable (and therefore easily remembered) image; one that is manageable, because it simplifies the complex nature of Nazism and the shattering history of the Third Reich, encapsulating them in the personality of Hitler; and one which constitutes 'myth', in the sense that we impose upon events (in past times and our own) particular interpretations whose truthfulness can never be beyond challenge.

Gombrich's comment is a good starting point from which to consider what is distinctive about cartoons as historical evidence. In offering an instant day-by-day interpretation of events, they resemble the news and feature columns among which they appear. If they go further and offer *approval* – more often disapproval – they perform a similar task to the newspaper 'editorial'. In the USA, indeed, they are habitually known as 'editorial cartoons'.

The cartoon is thus a particular kind of documentary evidence of what seems important at the time – a cartoonist's personal view of what people make of things. It gets its distinctiveness, of course, from working chiefly through pictures, not words. In caricature, words are dispensed with altogether: the reader is left to infer the person's character from those features which the cartoonist chooses to emphasise by exaggeration and distortion. Low drew Hitler with the trappings of dictatorship and military power, but diminished him as a threat by highlighting ridiculous (to the British) features such as his moustache. Again, Vicky (1913–66) hoped to make Harold Macmillan ridiculous, at the height of his prime ministerial power, by guying him as 'Supermac' – a joke which backfired (page 59).

Even when a cartoon incorporates a caption, it cannot make its point by argument. The cartoon's meaning is typically implicit: readers have

'But the old horse *must* go in front! Do you want to hurt his feelings?'

'The price of petrol has been increased by one penny' – Official.
(This cartoon, one of a series against Black Marketeers, was considered by the government to be detrimental to morale. The *Daily Mirror* was officially warned.)

'Funny way to run a battle'

to work it out for themselves. By comparison with an editorial, the cartoon is therefore blunt, assertive, shorn of qualification. It gives opinions, not reasons. All these characteristics, too, make it appeal first to the emotions, then (if at all) to the intellect. With a suitable image, the cartoonist can express, and evoke, a strength of revulsion beyond words against, say, a Hitler or a holocaust. Cartoonists have generally had more bite, and felt more comfortable, in contentious times and when they can be *against* things.

Cartoon metaphors

'Suitable image' is the key. The cartoonist's art is to find the right comparison to make his point. Election cartoons are full of the imagery of battles (page 60) and landslides – verbal metaphors adapted to a graphic form. Animal metaphors are always common: Low drew the TUC as a well-intentioned but lumbering carthorse (page 59). In the 1983 general election, politicians were drawn as horses, dogs, foxes, goats, sheep and deer. Mrs Thatcher appeared, too, as a cowboy, jockey, charioteer, hurdler, school ma'am, matron, pilot, surgeon and mountaineer. Historical, literary, screen and artistic analogies are also common: Vicky's 'Supermac' came from a science-fiction comic strip. Contemporary events can also serve as metaphors: the 1982 Falklands Task Force was relaunched in the 1983 election campaign as a fleet of Tory newspapers sailing to fight for Mrs Thatcher.

Simply to enumerate these features indicates the strength and weaknesses of cartoons as evidence. Certainly they give us a view of people's reaction to events. But if the view is largely *implied*, our own scope for misunderstanding is enormous. Moreover, if cartoons work by making comparisons, we need to understand the nuances of the thing to which the cartoon subject is compared. Policemen were caricatured as pigs in the 1970s: will pigs have the same resonance in the future for historians as they have for us today?

Beyond that, cartoons are likely not just to simplify but to *over*simplify. They overemphasise the importance of individuals rather than groups and organisations, and of people rather than ideas and impersonal forces. They concentrate on the national and international subjects dominating the national press, and they tend to neglect the parochial.

Humour and irony are risky weapons too. Humour works by comparison: we laugh at some things because we see resemblances and at others because we see contrasts. Old *Punch* cartoons are notorious for not now being funny. Cartoons depending on ridicule may lose their value if the humour becomes inaccessible. Irony is especially risky because it assumes readers will realise they are supposed to understand the opposite of what the cartoon seems to intend. This was

Vicky's problem with 'Supermac'. The tag was intended derisively (Aneurin Bevan had referred to Macmillan scathingly as 'MacWonder'), but it was seized on by Tories, and it stuck. In the 1959 election the nickname was one of Macmillan's main assets.

Misunderstood cartoons

Another cartoon famously misunderstood – a small historical event in its own right, like 'Supermac' – was Zec's *Daily Mirror* cartoon in the dark days of 1942 (page 60). Prime Minister Churchill interpreted it to mean that sailors' lives were being sacrificed to the profit of oil companies. Despite explaining that Zec meant 'save petrol, it costs lives', the paper was briefly in danger of being banned.

The historian studying Vicky's Supermac, or Low's Hitler and TUC carthorse, must thus beware of a variety of possible misunderstandings. What exactly does the Supermac cartoon show? That Macmillan at that time was a political superman? Or that he symbolised a post-war social and economic transformation, rather than being a superman himself? That Vicky believed he was one or other of those things? Or that Vicky believed he was not – but realised many other people thought he was? And so on. To this might be added a minor detail about the nuances of the caption references to 'Supermanship'. This was part of the title ('Supermanship', or, 'How to Continue to Stay Top Without Actually Falling Apart') of the latest book by the humorist Stephen Potter, inventor of 'gamesmanship', who was then in vogue. Its theme, which suited Vicky's irony, was how to give the appearance of achievement without the reality.

What this all amounts to, perhaps, is that the cartoon can be slippery evidence unless it is kept carefully within its proper context. Yet even if it is mainly subsidiary and corroborative, its images can be of enduring force, confirming in their own way the old adage that one picture is worth a thousand words.

Colin Seymour-Ure is Professor of Government at the University of Kent and Liz Ottaway is joint author of *Vicky* (Secker and Warburg, 1987).

Brian Harrison
Photographs

Brian Harrison describes the social impact of photography and analyses its uses and drawbacks as a historical source.

Photography became so easy and cheap during the 1880s that even children joined in. Charterhouse School's photographic club, founded in 1884, made three rooms available and provided lockers and shelves for members' equipment. Several public schools had similar clubs by the middle of the decade and, in November 1889, *Boys' Own Paper* offered its readers five guineas for the best set of six photographs sent in during the following eight months. So popular was the competition that the deadline was extended and the prize-money increased. In May 1890 the paper set up a *Boys' Own* postal photographic club to encourage the exchange of ideas, and during the following year it published several technical articles on the new art.

Photography had been growing fast since the census of 1851, when only 51 people called themselves photographers; by 1901 there were 17,268. Special photographic periodicals were launched in the 1850s and by the 1880s the idea of a 'National Photographic Portrait Gallery' was in the air. During that decade the *Photographic News* showed an infectious enthusiasm for this vigorous, thrusting new skill. The paper eagerly publicised new inventions and confidently predicted that tomorrow's discoveries would soon see off the problems of today. Amateur photography was also growing fast. It grew even faster after 1888 when George Eastman introduced the easily operated Kodak camera. By 1905 the camera was being used by one in ten of the population.[1] Thus any historian who writes about British history since 1880 must include the photograph with his other raw material – if only because the history of the media is as important as any other aspect of British social history.

But photographs do more than merely document an important aspect of media history. They do for modern British history what the aristocratic painting, the mosaic pavement or the discarded wine jar do for earlier periods – they help to document the history of society as a whole. At a time when a wide range of people are taking photographs (as in Britain since the 1880s), and where it is technically possible to record a broad span of human activity, the quantity, scope and quality of visual evidence is transformed.

The earliest photographs, which date from the early nineteenth century, cover only a very small range of human behaviour because they required skill, patience and wealth from the photographer. Cameras were first used in wartime during the Crimean War, but they could not yet capture the full horrors of war in the 1850s. Thereafter exposure times fell, tripods were slowly discarded, and by 1881 the *British Journal of Photography* thought photographs would soon be processed so quickly that the reporter-photographer would eventually oust the war artist.

In the same year the camera first revealed how birds fly. In 1882 the Prince of Wales was present at the Royal Institution with four princesses and a duke when Edward Muybridge used his photographs to show how incorrectly artists had hitherto portrayed the movements of a racehorse. The first photofinish in a race occurred in 1888, when Ernest Marks set up an improvised darkroom at an American racecourse and handed the negative to the judges within three minutes. Flash photography became possible in 1886, and the Prince of Wales set the fashion for night photographs by posing at midnight after the opera. It was some decades before the camera could capture colour, and in later life Rebecca West recalled how impossible it was for black-and-white photographs to convey the beauty of an Edwardian suffragette such as Christabel Pankhurst: 'She'd this wonderful colouring , marvellous colouring, and this extraordinary grace. Photography just lagged behind'. That problem, too, the twentieth century was able to solve.[2]

The camera's social impact

The camera has transformed the way we behave. It has substituted the pursuit of publicity for the cultivation of reticence. Frank Sutcliffe, the well-known late-Victorian photographer in Whitby, came across many local people who thought it unlucky to be drawn or photographed in any way. This attitude is now completely foreign to us. During the 1880s the camera increased the pressures of publicity in public life. At the general election of 1880, portraits of the local candidates were projected by magic lantern in at least one London borough, and at the general election of 1886 Gladstone's portrait was given to many constituents. Photographs of late-Victorian high church leaders in their full canonicals were distributed widely within the local diocese. Photographs of cabinet ministers were widely exhibited in late-Victorian shop windows, so that public celebrities could no longer travel about unobserved. So persistently did photographers pursue the politician, Lord Randolph Churchill, during his trip abroad in 1886 that the *Daily Telegraph* thought public figures would henceforth 'have to "make up" before they are allowed to drink in peace from any healing spring or lounge at ease in any kursaal or café'. The Prince of Wales soon grasped the new medium's potential. When opening Putney Bridge in 1886, he and the Princess were seen obediently to comply several times with the photographers' command: 'now then, quite still, if you please'.[3]

Always eager to advertise the camera's achievements, the *Photographic News*, discussing in 1884 'What Photography does for Science', pointed out that photography was nowadays 'a maid-of-all-work, put upon on every occasion, to discharge all sorts of functions, whether menial or high-class'. Prison governors by the 1850s were systematically photographing their prisoners, and by the 1880s the case-books of asylums and the library of Scotland Yard collected photographs of lunatics and criminals. By 1886, photographs of MPs were even helping the police to exclude unauthorised people from entering the House of Commons.

In so far as photography was being built into the process of nineteenth-century research, it was bound eventually to assist historians of much earlier periods. The Ordnance Survey experimented with photography in map-making during the 1850s, and with the twentieth-century advent of air survey photography the camera contributed massively to the archaeology of all periods from the prehistoric onwards. O.G.S. Crawford's achievement should by noted here, with his publication in 1924 of the Ordnance Survey's *Map of Roman Britain* in its first edition.

The photograph as a historical source: a critique

The camera did not immediately transform the way people looked at the world for at least two reasons: earlier artistic conventions profoundly influenced the professional and amateur photographer's choice and interpretation of his subject just as they influenced the way photographs were viewed by the general public. Frank Sutcliffe's photographic style, for instance, owes much to the French painter J.F. Millet. Photographs in every period reflect the artistic convention of the day, and this is especially true of nineteenth-century Britain. All the well-known Victorian photographers had earlier been artists or had received artistic training. The debate on whether photography is an art or a science was vigorous throughout the nineteenth century and remains lively today. Some early photographers thought that the noblest outlet for their skill was merely to reproduce works of creative art, and many more viewed their photographs primarily as artistic creations. 'We photographers have no Constables, no Whistlers', wrote Sutcliffe in 1916. 'So the student had better not look at photographs after all till his taste is perfectly broken in. It will be safer for him to look at pictures'.[4]

Artistic convention is not the only barrier between the camera and reality. To begin with, the historian must beware of forgeries. The trial of Graham Ovenden in 1980 showed that the rising price fetched by Victorian photographs had brought many forgeries on to the market.[5] Contemporaries practised milder forms of photographic deception: the *Photographic News* claimed in 1886 that photographs of the Queen in state robes were misleading because she was standing on a concealed box. Everyone who knows they are going to be photographed wants to look at their best, and the sort of photograph that tends to survive is the formal record of a special event.

People get themselves photographed more as they want to be remembered than as they usually are. They tend only to photograph what is exceptional and therefore striking – not those recurring day-to-day and relatively uninteresting things that mould our lives so much more profoundly. It is no accident that there was an outburst of photography in connection with the jubilee of 1887, just as in 1953 it was the coronation which firmly rooted television into the British home. The camera is brought out for staged occasions, especially for those family functions (weddings, christenings, funerals) where people geographically scattered or generationally divided can for a brief moment be captured together. Reinforced by the family album, the camera has helped to infuse history with nostalgia, especially as so many early photographs could be taken only in fine weather.

The very act of taking a photograph alters the conduct of those who know they are being observed. Some aspects of human behaviour are (for reasons quite other than technical) inherently inaccessible to the camera – the essence of the political process, for example, and the intimacies of spiritual and intellectual activity. A cabinet may be photographed in session, but not the intricacies of the political process that are central to its function. Again, the unexpected event rarely finds the photographer on the spot – the assassination of Lord Frederick Cavendish in Phoenix Park in 1882, for example, or the IRA's blowing up of Airey Neave in 1979. Neave's death does, however, illustrate how conventions change on what it is legitimate for the photographer to record. Cameramen in 1979 showed no Victorian scruple: during the election campaign they enhanced the cruelty of public life by pursuing Mrs Thatcher for her instant reaction to the death of a much-respected supporter.

So the camera is not neutral in recording the past: it is operated by a photographer who is deeply influenced by contemporary ideas about what ought to be photographed and how. The photograph is less a window giving a clear and comprehensive view of past reality than a mirror reflecting back into the present the long-lost values and inhibitions of the past. These values and inhibitions are themselves important raw material for the historian who wishes to explain how the past differs from the present, but such influences can be high-lighted only by non-photographic types of source. Only the printed or manuscript document, for instance, can tell us that when Frank Sutcliffe photographed boys bathing nude at Whitby in his famous 'Water Rats' of 1886, much local scandal was caused by his choice of subject-matter. He also found it difficult to persuade local working people to be photographed while working: 'laundrymaids hanging out sheets, and carrying heavy baskets of clothes', he wrote in 1914, 'would make grand subjects if laundrymaids had not such objections to being photographed in anything but their Sunday garments'.[6]

Furthermore the photographer, however skilful, can illuminate aspects of society accessible to only one of our five senses – the eye – and precious little even of that. It can tell us nothing about noise, smell, touch and taste. It has marked limitations even in portraiture. 'Photography was always a little unkind to Mrs Langtry's type of beauty', wrote *Photographic News* in 1885: 'The camera is powerless where fascination of manner and charms of conversation are con-cerned'.[7] A historian can no more concentrate exclusively on 'visual history' – on a type of history that grows purely out of visual types of evidence – than on 'oral history', 'documentary history' or 'archaeo-logical history'. History is, as Isaiah Berlin once said, 'a rich brew', and its full richness will be available only after every relevant type of source has been drawn upon for the task in hand.

Nonetheless, the historian of Britain since the 1880s has to incorpo-rate the photograph into his raw material. For all the camera's distor-tions of reality, its powers of accurate representation forced it to the forefront, and artists had to respond. High-speed photography demonstrated how the legs of fast-moving animals really move; the portrait painter now required fewer sittings from his subject; and aris-tocratic good looks could no longer survive challenge from below. The camera helped to create a sort of meritocracy of beauty whereby 'pro-fessional beauties' of humbler birth – Lily Langtry, Mrs Cornwallis-West, Mrs Luke Wheeler – came to the fore. Indeed, so feeble was the artist's power of representation that in the twentieth century he largely vacated the field of representation to the camera, and retreated into the realms of imagination and abstraction: he would in future found his professional status on doing what the camera could not do.

There is one more reason why the historian will embrace the photo-graph. For him and his readers it can clarify more vividly than any prose and more accurately than any painting or drawing just how the past differs from the present. It is important for the historian not just to explain what the past was like, but also to ensure that his explanation makes an impact on hearers and readers. Here the photograph's immediacy and relative authenticity help immensely. The many systematic photographic collections on long-lost buildings more vividly evoke the mood of Victorian city and slum than any other source. The historian who studies P.H. Emerson's scenes of country life in late-Victorian Norfolk or Henry Taunt's street scenes in early twentieth-century Oxford will describe those two communities with greatly enhanced insight. The photograph stirs the imagination, and rare indeed is the modern, or even the ancient, historian who can afford to ignore it.

Notes

(1) Statistics from Gernsheim, H. and A. *History of Photography ... up to 1914* (Oxford University Press, 1955) p. 166; Martin, G. H. and Francis, D. 'The camera's eye', in H. J. Dyos and M. Wolff (eds), *The Victorian City, I* (Routledge and Kegan Paul, 1973) p. 241.

(2) Author's interview with Dame Rebecca West at 48, Kingston House North, Princes' Gate, London, SW7 on 15 August 1974.

(3) *Daily Telegraph*, 29 October 1886, p. 4. *Daily News* quoted in *Photographic News*, 4 June 1886, p.360.

(4) Hiley, M. *Frank Sutcliffe* (Gordon Fraser Gallery, 1974) p. 87. On the relationship between art and photography, see Aaron Scharf's admirable *Art and Photography* (2nd edn, Penguin, 1974).

(5) See Hooper, J. 'The art of the authentic', *Guardian*, 22 November 1980, p. 17.

(6) Hiley op.cit., p. 62.

(7) *Photographic News*, 22 May 1885, p. 328.

Brian Harrison teaches History at the University of Oxford. Among his many books and articles on modern British social and political history is *A Hundred Years Ago: Britain in the 1880s in Words and Photographs* (Penguin Books, 1983), which he co-authored with Colin Ford.

Maxwell G. Lee and Terry Wyke
Maps

*Maps cannot only prove valuable illustrations or a guide to the course of
military campaigns; they are also a major source of information in themselves
and a record of changing perceptions of the areas and subjects represented.*

As historical events take place in space as well as time, few historians
would argue that their task of interpretation is not aided by an understanding of geography. Historians and geographers have pointed to
the symbolic relationship which exists between their disciplines. Sir
John Clapham's observation:

> He is a very imperfect economic historian who is not a tolerable geo-
> grapher; and I cannot picture to myself a useful historical geogra-
> pher who has not a fair working knowledge of economic history.

This could be matched by similar statements going back to the seventeenth century. Yet, in spite of exhortations for historians to understand more about the stage on which the drama of history is played
out, and the emergence of disciplines like historical geography, it is
evident that the relationship is not always as close as it ought to be.

A valuable tool

Maps represent one of the most central and accessible tools provided
by geography, yet it is clear that history students from primary school
to higher education often fail to make effective use of them in their
studies. Unsurprisingly, a similar neglect is evident among academic
historians. An examination of the content and bibliographies of a large
sample of recently-published history books, both texts and mono-
graphs on European history covering all periods, points to the conclu-
sion that maps are not included regularly, or, it would appear,
consulted. Certainly, when maps are included, and the majority of
books manage without them, they often appear to be an afterthought
rather than an integral part of the study. They are less likely to be used
as a tool to explain or advance a line of argument preferring to remain
descriptive, identifying political boundaries, settlements and the like.
However, this use should not be denigrated, given the evidence from
recent surveys of the extensive ignorance about the location of countries in the modern world that exists among both American and
European students. It is a sad thought that although centuries of map-

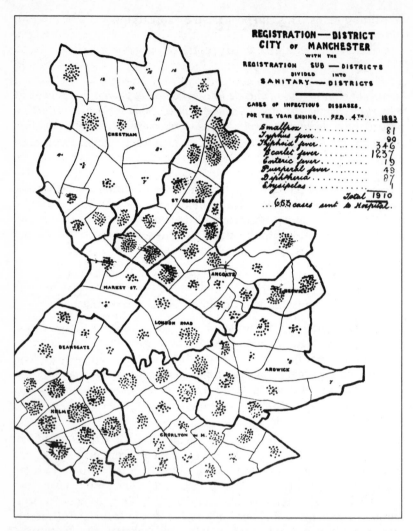

An outline map of Manchester with the Registration Sub-districts divided into Sanitary districts. Showing cases of infectious diseases in part of the city for the year ending 4 February 1883.

making have altered our perception of the known world, many continents appear to remain *terra incognita* to a large section of the present-day educated public.

Historians who do not make use of map evidence tend to isolate themselves and their students from a valuable source of information. All history students should be encouraged to develop the habit of consulting maps. This can be started by consulting modern maps of those countries, regions or cities being studied. Students undertaking a particular study, of Japan for example, ought to spend a brief period examining a physical relief map of the Japanese islands which would give them some appreciation of the land-use and patterns of rural and urban development as well as the problems of communication and transport planning. Detailed geological maps will provide information about both solid and drift deposits which help in an appreciation of the pattern of settlement location and the potential and actual uses of an area. The availability or absence of particular building materials, for instance, frequently plays a part in determining where people have chosen to live. This use of modern maps should demonstrate quickly to the student that maps are a unique source of material, providing in a succinct manner, a considerable volume of evidence which is not easily available in other forms.

A rich source

However, it is in the study of historical maps that the historian will find just how rich a vein of source material is available. Students embarking on a study of African history will find their understanding deepened if at an early stage they discover how the mapping of the continent altered perceptions, especially European, about it. To trace the cartographic history of Africa, say from John Blaeu's map of 1635 to the colonial maps of the early twentieth century is to open an important perspective on the continent's history which can then be complemented by reference to more conventional sources:

> So Geographers in Afric maps,
> With Savage Pictures fill their gaps,
> and O'er unhabitable Downs
> Place Elephants for Want of Towns.
> **(Swift, 1733)**

Britain is particularly rich in maps and the historian can consult a wide range of printed maps covering the whole country, whole counties and towns from the sixteenth century onwards. Printed maps produced for a specific purpose such as those which accompany the enclosure of a village, or for the tithe compilation in the 1830s are also available as, of course, are an extensive range of manuscript plans and maps. Depending on the questions being examined, such maps may provide an invaluable source of evidence.

Types of map

Probably the most familiar maps covering Britain are those produced by the Ordnance Survey. As the name suggest these originated for military purposes, a significant factor in the early history of mapmaking. It was the fear of invasion from the continent which led the British government to initiate the survey undertaken by the Board of Ordnance which was eventually to produce the first systematic and consistent mapping of the country. During the nineteenth century the national Ordnance Survey maps were regularly revised using a larger scale (6 inches and 25 inches to the mile). The need to provide accurate, large-scale maps of towns, particularly for sanitary engineering purposes, also led the Ordnance Survey to provide urban maps on a scale of 60 inches and, later, 120 inches to the mile from the 1840s onwards. The level of detail on these large-scale urban maps never fails to surprise those who consult them for the first time.

Apart from the identification of buildings, other urban features mapped include water pumps, lamp posts, pillar boxes and even trees. By consulting maps of the same area surveyed at different times during the century it is possible to build up an understanding very quickly of aspects of the process of urban development. This can be extended by studying other large-scale urban maps, such as those produced for fire insurance from the 1880s onwards, by Charles Goad. To this day, the company of that name continues to produce large-scale maps of city centres. Another useful group of large-scale maps are those underground maps produced in connection with the development of water, gas and electricity systems in British cities. Like the Goad maps they can often fill in information about urban land-use for periods when the large-scale ordnance survey plans were not revised.

As with any type of historical source, maps need to be used critically. The source of maps needs to be established; answers need to be supplied to the questions of why and how particular maps were produced. The year(s) when an area was surveyed needs to be considered, particularly for maps that pre-date the twentieth century, and attention given to when a particular map was published. Before 1850 there was often a considerable gestation period between surveying and publication, of which historians need to be aware. As they were expensive items to produce, there was often much pirating and borrowing of cartographic material which should also make one cautious of accepting unquestioningly the publication date of maps. Fortunately, there are a number of books on the history of mapmaking which will help.

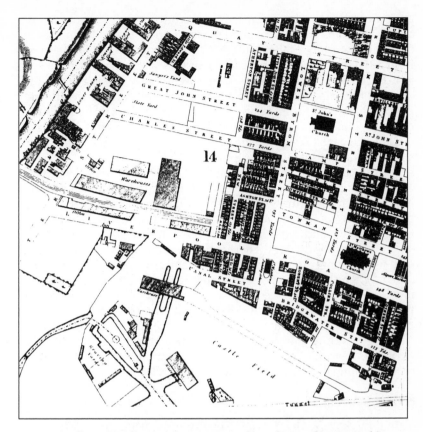

An extract from Banks and Company's plan of Manchester and its environs from a survey completed in 1831 at a scale of 1:3,600. It shows the site of the Roman Fort at Castlefield and the terminus of the first passenger railway line between Liverpool and Manchester's Liverpool Road.

Analysis of social data

In the nineteenth century maps were not confined simply to providing evidence of physical and man-made features but they were used increasingly by social researchers as a tool to present and analyse social data. British public health reformers, following continental examples, began to use maps to show the impact of the first cholera epidemic in 1831–2. By the time of the third cholera epidemic, John Snow was using a well-established method of analysing social data when he produced his well-known map of the cholera outbreak in Soho. Social reformers also appreciated the value of maps in spreading their messages: the temperance lobby producing a large number of anti-drink maps which identified the location of licensed premises in cities like London, Manchester, York and Oxford. One of the most influential uses of maps by a social researcher was the poverty maps which Charles Booth used to summarise, in an accessible form, the detailed findings uncovered in his monumental study of wealth and poverty in late Victorian London. The mapping of social data has not ceased in this century, yet it is surprising how infrequently historians use it as a means to describe the spatial distribution of phenomena let alone explore causal relationships.

It is our contention that historians need to use maps more systematically. They need to be consulted in the reconnaissance stage of any new research as naturally as one might use an encyclopaedia. They have to be used with an appreciation of their limitations, but when used critically and supported with other forms of evidence, their strengths become evident. There is no hierarchy in the sources available to historians, their usefulness depends on the questions being asked. When answering particular questions visual sources like maps in addition to such sources as paintings, cartoons, photographs and film, can provide essential information and prompt insights which the written word cannot supply. The old adage that 'history is about chaps, geography is about maps' will increasingly be shown to be wrong, as historians and geographers co-operate in a closer alliance, each accepting that their sources are equally relevant to the other.

Further Reading

Harley, J.B. *Maps for the Local Historian* (Bedford Square Press, 1972).
Harley, J.B. *Ordnance Survey Maps – A Descriptive Manual* (Ordnance Survey, 1975).
Hindle, B.P. *Maps for Local History* (B.T. Batsford, 1988).
Smith, D. *Maps and Plans for the Local Historian and Collector* (B.T. Batsford, 1988).

Maxwell G. Lee recently retired as Lecturer in Urban and Historical Geography whilst Terry Wyke is a Lecturer in Economic History at Manchester Metropolitan University.

Arthur Marwick
Art

Art is a complex source to use; its context and the circumstances of its creation must be taken into account. However, art can provide valuable insights into the metaphors and mores of the society in which it found expression.

The sources historians use vary according to the topic being studied. Paintings, sculptures, etchings, etc. are likely to be of most use in certain aspects of cultural and social history, and probably of least use in most branches of political, diplomatic and constitutional history. The question that must always be asked of any 'text' or 'artefact' being put forward as a source is 'does it tell us anything we didn't know already?' or, more probingly, 'does it tell us anything we couldn't discover more readily from a different source?' For example, a painting of eighteenth-century French peasants eating bread, garlic and wine may be evidence of their regular diet, but we would almost certainly be better to go to the written sources, household accounts, contemporary descriptions, etc.; and there is always the quite strong possibility that the artist might have been more concerned with infusing his painting with the religious symbolism of the Last Supper than with accurate sociological observation.

Flattering to deceive

Of all types of source material, artistic sources are most misused. It is perfectly legitimate for publishers to wish to brighten up books by including reproductions of various works of art. But, with rare exceptions, such works will, at best, be no more than illustrations; at worst they may have little real relevance to what is being said in the article or book. The key questions are 'did the author him- or herself actually make use of the work of art in composing the article or book, does he or she actually refer to them as would be the case with extracts from diaries or acts of parliament, or have the illustrations simply been stuck on as decoration, probably by someone else?'

Even the most austere political works sometimes contain portraits of the principal characters whose achievements and failings are being discussed, often boldly captioned 'Mary, Queen of Scots', 'Chatham', etc. Actually, of course, such portraits are merely representations of the sitters, more or less accurate likenesses depending upon the skill and the aims of the artist (was he a flatterer, did he have some idealised image of monarchy, or of women?). In some cases the sitter may not actually have been the person identified in the caption; there used to be dozens of paintings labelled Madame de Pompadour – now all the really good-looking ones are recognised as not being of La Pompadour at all. So: if we are to use portraits as sources for what historical personages really looked like, we have to analyse them, and the purposes of their creators, just as carefully as we would any other historical source, and likewise, take into account all the other (mainly written) evidence.

Reading the wrong message

A vital procedure with any source is establishing its date. A nineteenth-century painting of the compiling of a Domesday Book entry is quite worthless as a source for the study of Domesday Book, though it might well tell us much about nineteenth-century romanticisation of the Middle Ages. Recently, in the Boston Museum of Fine Arts, I was renewing acquaintanceship with Turner's *Slave Ship (Slavers Throwing Overboard the Dead and Dying, Typhoon Coming On)* of 1842, when I noticed in the caption the claim that this painting demonstrated Turner's active involvement in the anti-slavery campaign. Here dating is utterly crucial: the slave trade (which is what the picture relates to) was abolished in the British Empire in 1807 (and the institution of slavery in 1833) and indeed the incident on which Turner's painting was based took place in the late eighteenth century. Thus, though the painting may be taken as an example of what might be called 'retrospective radicalism' it cannot be an item in the active campaign against the slave trade. (The museum, I may say, has promptly and courteously corrected the error.)

Bringing paintings, cartoons, etc. into historical study is rather trendy and can be great fun. Recently, I gave the key-note address and the final summing up at a conference in the Netherlands devoted to the use of such 'images' in history. Some of the papers were brilliant, marshalling masses of written evidence in order to bring out the precise significance of certain 'images' – monuments to military victory in the eighteenth century for instance, the vanity and God-like assumptions of the French monarchy being contrasted with the Christian humility of the God-fearing Habsburgs. But some papers were sheer speculation: if you are going to discuss readers' reactions to newspaper cartoons, you have to look for the evidence (in letters to the editor, for example) – you can't just make them up. Another speaker fantasised about what popular and commercial art says about foreign perceptions of the Dutch. His naive wafflings about the Dutch being seen as a carefree, bucolic nation were crushed by an expert critic who demonstrated from a great range of other sources that the overwhelming perception foreigners have is of scrupulously clean and intensely industrious people. The speaker had been trying to fit his artistic sources to the wrong topic: what they did reveal, if interrogated properly, were assumptions behind the marketing of biscuits, cocoa, cheeses, etc. It is, alas, all too easy to impose propagandist meanings on artistic sources: this rural landscape represents the ruling class expropriating the peasantry (or, alternatively, the benign harmony of the perfectly integrated society), that domestic interior represents the suppression of women; they may do, but the points have to be argued with evidence external to the paintings themselves, not simply asserted.

Art in its context

Let me pick up again my references to the Last Supper and to nineteenth-century Romanticism. The presence of strong religious symbolism in a painting (requiring, naturally, experience and expertise to decode) will tell us a great deal about the belief system of an artist and his patrons. And with the 'isms' of history, we really are in business. It would be quite impossible to give a thorough account of English Romanticism at the end of the eighteenth century without analysing the paintings of Constable, Turner, Cotman and the water-colourists. It would be quite absurd to assess the strength of modernism in Britain before the First World War without reference to the paintings of Wyndham Lewis and C.R.W. Nevinson.

Here I am talking of élite art and cultural movements affecting the élite. But popular art (cartoons, woodcuts, etchings) can tell us much about the attitudes and values of wider sections of society, about mentalities, about ordinary folk and popular culture. R.W. Scribner's 'attempt to combine print and picture' in 'a study of visual propaganda, and of its role in the dissemination of the evangelical movement during the first half-century of the Reformation of Germany', entitled *For the Sake of the Simple Folk* (Cambridge, 1981), triumphantly vindicates his argument 'that through a study of visual propaganda we may gain a wider understanding of how the Reformation appealed to common folk than by concentrating attention more narrowly on printed propaganda alone'. On the lower quarters of the two facing pages 60–1, Scribner prints reproductions of two woodcuts (illustrations 43 and 44 respectively in the book); across the same two pages Scribner provides an absolutely precise analysis of these artistic sources, bringing out his main point that in the religious propaganda of the day great use was made of popular games:

> A good example can be found in the title page to the pamphlet *The Lutheran Strebkatz* (ill. 43) The Strebkatz was a popular game in

which two opponents engaged in a tug-of-war by gripping between their teeth two rods which were connected by chords. This contraption was itself called the Strebkatz and the players contended for its sole possession. In this version, the chords pass around the contestants' necks. The original form of the game is depicted in the title page of a 1522 pamphlet (ill. 44), where two monks contend for the prize, a wreathe held by a watching damsel. In the first instance, the contestants are Luther and the Pope, who is helped by a crowd of supporters representing some of Luther's main opponents – Eck, Emser, Cockleus, Murner, Hochstraten, Lemp and Alfeld. Although the contest seems unequal, Luther has dragged the Pope to his knees so violently that his tiara has fallen off and his money purse has burst.

You can see just how much detailed knowledge Scribner has to have in order to make use of the rich examples of popular art.

Art and culture

Evidently, great movements of ideas, such as the Reformation or the Renaissance, are areas for which artistic sources are bound to be extremely helpful. The distinguished Reformation scholar, A.G. Dickens, taking care to have the appropriate reproductions included in his book *The Age of Humanism and Reformation* (1972), used the evidence of the art and architecture of the time to contest the theory that seventeenth-century Baroque art and architecture was a product of the Catholic Reformation, 'a hymn of joy raised by the triumphant Church', closely associated with the Jesuits. The Baroque, he argued, using the artistic sources themselves, 'soon became a multi-purpose style contributing as much to the glorification of monarchs as to the triumph of the Church.'

In his *Italian Renaissance: Culture and Society in Italy* (1986), Peter Burke takes care to place his reproductions of the artistic sources exactly where he is analysing and discussing them in the text: thus they contribute to his argument in exactly the same way that quotations from written sources do. Another celebrated example of the use of art to give breathtaking insights into the mentalities of a particular society in a particular age is *The Embarrassment of Riches: An Interpretation of Dutch Culture in the Golden Age* (New York, 1987) by Simon Schama. Here is part of the analysis which runs beside and underneath the Jan Steen painting, *Tavern Scene* (p. 205):

As a source of bawdy innuendo, the pipe seems to have been inexhaustibly ribald .... One of the many tavern paintings to include a guffawing self-portrait is virtually an anthology of Dutch smut, no lewd reference to the condition of the girl or to the act which brought it about has been omitted. Broken egg shells, mussels, and open flap-kan tankard, a gaping bunghole, a scrutinised chamber pot and no fewer than three pointing handles and stems provide rib-nudging visual counterparts for the cruel prurience of the cacophonous laughter.

If we are interested in the way which science, technology and indus-trialisation came increasingly to dominate life in all of its aspects, cer-tain painters, from Joseph Wright of Derby (his *An Experiment on a Bird in an Air Pump*, c.1767, in the Tate, is well known) in the late eighteenth century to Fernand Léger in the twentieth, are helpful witnesses. If we are interested in the wider ramifications of the great revolutions in his-tory, we do well to pay heed, for example, to the classical modes of the French revolutionary artist David, which postulate that the Revolution has brought a restoration of the values of Ancient Rome; likewise to the way in which, in post-revolutionary Russia, experimental and modernistic 'constructivism' quickly gave way to tedious and banal 'social realism'.

Conclusion

Portraits, carefully analysed, can be psychologically very penetrating. Certain landscapes and townscapes can be very useful for topography, for what places used to look like: one can practically plot the geographi-cal expansion and transformation of Paris from the remarkable series of paintings now collected in the new extension to the Musée Carnavalet. Yet other genres can be helpful on questions of dress and fashion, and if read carefully, and in conjunction with the other evidence, on the matter of social distinctions – some of the early eighteenth-century French painters, and many of the Victorians are useful here.

For the historian studying an entire period, say the 'Belle Epoque' (1890–1914) or the 1960s, the art of the period may well be a vital source. Though Aubrey Beardsley, Bonnard and Vuillard, the early Balla, each had his own artistic purposes, the common denominators, once they have been deciphered, speak volumes on the characteristic contradictions of the era: innovation and decadence, complacency and uncertainty, the arrogance of unconstrained wealth and the degrada-tion of unmitigated poverty. In their use of discarded objects and materials, both Nouveau Realisme and Arte Povera are joined to Pop Art in an intimate and revealing relationship to the exploding con-sumerism of the 1960s and reactions to it. History is the study of human activities in all their immense variety. Artistic sources are not the easiest to read, but in all sorts of ways they are among the richest.

Arthur Marwick is Professor of History at the Open University.

M. H. Port
Architecture and the Townscape

The archaeologist is familiar with the problem of making stones sing; but for the historian, too, buildings can augment, or even supply the want of, the written word. To read them one has to acquire certain skills, just as one has to master the language and writing of written documents.

Determination of the building type helps set the context. Some types are immediately obvious: church, town house, country house. But today railway stations or churches have sometimes been converted to residential use. Some building types that have endured for centuries may well require a more exact classification: the town house, for example – detached, semi-detached, or terraced. Others, such as the stone castle, have had a limited life; or have only appeared in the last two centuries, for example the railway station.

A government office will seldom have been built before governmental activities expanded into the ordinary life of the citizen, from the mid-nineteenth century onwards. The purpose-built bank originated when wealth had become relatively widely diffused and money transactions widespread and complex, but often requiring the presence of individuals concerned in the transaction. To give people confidence to use them, banks had to show that they were financially sound, so they constructed impressive buildings of noble architecture in prominent locations.

Let us look at a building type in greater detail: the parish church is a familiar one. What has happened to it over the centuries since it was built, possibly in the twelfth century? Changes in religious ideas that were reflected in the design of churches occurred even before the Reformation. For example, the cult of masses for the dead led to a multiplication of altars and the building of chapels to accommodate them. Rich men sought insurance against hellfire by improving their parish church, thereby also winning the goodwill of the parishioners, whose principal meeting-place it was. In towns, gilds and confraternities built and maintained their own chapels, humble or splendid according to their wealth. Thus work of different periods (distinguished by different styles) is found in one church, and from it we can learn a good deal about the character of the community over a long period.

Most towns have several churches. After the Reformation few were built for some 250 years. By the early nineteenth century, the increase in population and its changing distribution meant there was a lack of churches. Many were in need of structural repair while, at the same time, internal furnishings that had accumulated over the previous two centuries, particularly in the way of enclosed seats ('pews') for local landowners, were antipathetic to a changing social ethos and changing liturgical patterns. Many people had turned away from the state church, and nonconformist chapels sprang up. In the nineteenth century many new churches and chapels were built, reflecting the central role of religion in national life; but representing a diversity of forms of Christianity, including the return of Roman Catholicism. Old churches were modernised, by both 'restoration' of their structure, and changes in arrangement to meet changing liturgical ideas. The restorers frequently tried not merely to mend but also to perfect; substituting a design of some ideal period for what was actually there. A fifteenth-century window, for instance, (regarded as decadent) might be replaced by a copy of a thirteenth-century window. This makes the 'reading' of an old parish church a task full of pitfalls.

A knowledge of the social history of a period helps in relating buildings to their environment. But we are asking the reciprocal question, what light do buildings throw on their environment? To tackle that with more precision, we must analyse the component factors. First there is the plan of the building, how it is set out on the ground, the functions and relationship of its various rooms. Then there is the style in which it is built, the outward form and the internal decoration. Thirdly, we need to consider the constructional elements: what keeps a building standing?

(a) The plan

The plan of a building may throw light on social usages and structures. Take a row of back-to-back cottages in, say, Leeds or Nottingham, each with its own door to the street and consisting of two floors, with one room about ten feet square on each. What can we learn from the plan? Each unit was designed for a 'household': probably consisting of a husband, wife and children. The plan reduces both site-cost and building-cost to a minimum, with no garden , yard, or passages at side or back of any cottage, every wall save that on the street serving two units. Clearly these units were designed for renting by the poor.

How would such a household use its space? The existence of two rooms suggests a division into the basic functions of daily living and sleeping; no further differentiation would be possible. Need might even drive them to rent out one room to a second household, whether individual lodger or family. Such houses would have been constructed when there was a keen demand for living accommodation from the poor, so we can relate them to a time when there was an influx

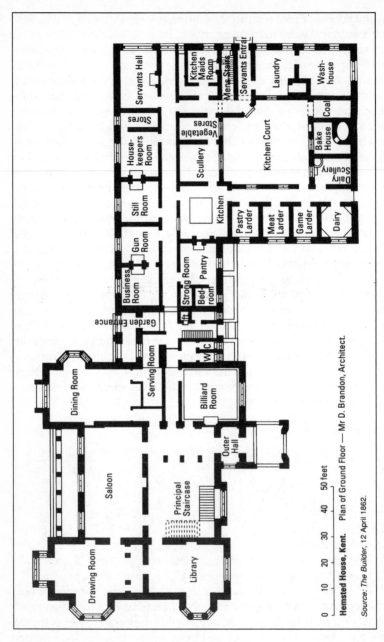

Hemsted House, Kent. Plan of Ground Floor — Mr D. Brandon, Architect.

Source: The Builder, 12 April 1862.

Plan of the ground floor of Hemsted House, Kent. Its sheer scale indicates a rich lifestyle.

into the towns. Furthermore they were intended for someone who would pay rent regularly every week. Factory workers drawn into towns by the industrial developments of the late eighteenth and early nineteenth centuries fit the description. The other factors: style (or rather its absence: merely walls, roofs, doors and windows), and construction – the flimsiest of walls, of cheap brick, with cheap slate roofs of low pitch – go to support the evidence of the plan.

In stark contrast, the large country house by its sheer scale indicates a rich lifestyle, supported by troops of servants. The many rooms had clearly differentiated functions. One was for eating in, or even specifically for the formal evening dinner, eaten in special costume. Other meals might be taken less formally in the breakfast or morning room. Rooms were set aside for specific leisure pursuits: billiards required space and good lighting. A smoking room indicates a society in which the habit, though allowable, was not acceptable to everyone. The library suggests intellectual life, or the need to pretend to it; a gun-room, country sports. The range of intercommunicating reception rooms offers scope for large-scale entertaining.

All these things suggest a sizeable leisured and wealthy class. It functioned by means of numerous servants, highly organised, as can be seen by the serving wing, distanced from the main rooms. Three departments – cook, housekeeper and butler, each with appropriate staff – can be identified, with the rooms of male and female servants carefully segregated, access controlled by butler and housekeeper respectively. Laundry and brewhouse, well removed from the main house because of the unpleasant smells they generated, were needed before these services were available commercially. Stables, equally removed from the main house again because of their offensive smell, indicate a period dependent on the horse for transport.

Such highly-articulated houses were built in the mid-nineteenth century, when there was plenty of labour willing to service this highly artificial social construct. Similar houses of an earlier or later date generally afford a simpler service wing, and the principal rooms themselves tend to be more multi-functional. Another clue to date is the placing of the main rooms on the first floor in the early Georgian period.

(b) Style

Architecture has two basic levels: vernacular, put up according to traditional practices, but having some element of 'delight', some architectural character, and 'polite', devised by a design specialist. Today most buildings are designed by professionals, but in, say, the seventeenth century, only the more important buildings were, so that vernacular architecture reached higher up the social scale. It slowly assimilated the changing fashions that marked polite architecture. Thus, windows developed from a range of rectangular lights to a range of taller lights divided horizontally, and gradually glazed; thence to a series of two-light, squarish windows, opening either by horizontally sliding sashes or side-hung casements, with a grid of glazing bars; and so, about the end of the seventeenth century, to the tall rectangle of the vertically-sliding sash window. External appearance is evidence as to the date of even a humble building, while for more important buildings one has a well-established stylistic chronology.

(c) Construction

Basically, there are two structural systems: 'mass', that of load-bearing walls; and 'frame' (essentially the system of the skyscraper) in which the loads of roof and floors are carried down to the foundation by a frame, which is then clad, or in-filled by some weather-tight material. Recent research into the details of wooden-frame construction has revealed much about its technical developments, such as the forms of joints between the roofing timbers, and chronologies have been proposed.

Wooden-frame construction was somewhat superseded as brick became a universal building material in the late seventeenth century (though wood was often employed to give rigidity to the brickwork). Old framed houses were often given a new front constructed in brick. But with the need for large open-span buildings in the industrial revolution, framing came back into favour, the first multi-storeyed iron-framed building ever erected dating from 1796.

Similarly with walling, the techniques employed give clues as to date and social hierarchy. Stone was noble, but where readily available it was often used as the common building material, even for such utilitarian features as barns. But this was generally 'rubble' walling, the natural face of the stone, or roughly hammered, laid irregularly or roughly squared. For high-quality work the stone had to be dressed by the mason to obtain a smooth surface and regularly shaped block, termed 'ashlar'.

Bricks may tell even more than stone. Although available, they were not widely used before the sixteenth century. They were handmade on site, where the earth was suitable. There was accordingly a great deal of variation. But as bricks were prescribed for the rebuilding of the city after the Great Fire of London, the authorities endeavoured to impose quality controls. The red brick prevalent in late Stuart days proved too fierce a colour for mid-Georgian taste, and by the later eighteenth century the high-quality yellowish-purple London stock brick had become the general walling material of the metropolis. About 1870 red brick returned to fashion in London, as parts of Mayfair show. From

1784 to 1850 an excise tax on bricks imposed a uniformity which gave a new regularity to brick walling. After the lifting of the tax, the new railway network facilitated centralising brick production in areas such as Bedfordshire, where the earth was particularly suitable.

Not only the type and size of brick give clues as to its date, but also the method of laying the brick. A loadbearing brick wall generally needs to be at least two bricks in thickness. Bricks being twice as long as wide, a substantial wall may be readily constructed with some laid lengthways and others crossways. The oldest method was to lay the bricks at random; subsequently 'English bond', alternate rows of 'headers' and 'stretchers', was commonly employed. By the eighteenth century, 'Flemish bond' was popular, headers and stretchers alternating both horizontally and vertically. The nineteenth century saw a return to the late medieval fashion of using coloured bricks to form patterns, or simply in a row as a string-course.

Townscape

By examining the plan, the style and the construction of a building we can not merely date it, but learn about the sort of people who lived in or used it, the way in which they used it, and the esteem in which it was held. Putting together the studies of individual buildings as they stand in the townscape, we can see how changes occurred. In Ludlow, for example, a profitable cloth industry, and the manufacture of arrows and gloves, had created a prosperous bourgeoisie that had built the largest parish church in Shropshire, its soaring fifteenth-century tower paid for by the gilds, a grammar school, alms-houses, as well as fine half-timbered frame houses. In 1536 Ludlow became the seat of the Council in the Marches of Wales, which brought it much administrative and legal business. But the Council's abolition in 1689 and the loss of the cloth trade to more successful rivals led to a decline, from which it was rescued by the development of glove manufacture, trade in malt, and the local country gentry's coming to spend at least the winter in the town. Brick houses or facades appeared; a distinct high-quality residential area was carved out; public walks were laid out, a theatre established, entertainments – assemblies and race-meetings – provided. To this social history, the buildings of the town bear witness.

M. H. Port is Emeritus Professor of History at Queen Mary and Westfield College, London.

Sam Merry
Novels

Contemporary novels can be extremely evocative of the period studied. But how accurate are they as historical documents?

Novels are very useful to historians, but they need to be treated with great care before they yield their evidence. They are works of fiction whose primary purpose is to entertain. They must contain a plot, in which characters operate against a setting. This setting is determined by the nature of the novel: it may be deliberately historical as in the historical novel, or it may be historical in the sense that the novelist has chosen to position the setting in a time which is distant from his or her own. Or it may be historical in the sense that the time at which the novelist was writing has now become distanced by the passage of time.

This raises the question as to whether novels are primary or secondary sources, and in particular whether historical novels should be treated as primary or secondary evidence. Primary and secondary sources become such according to what use the historian puts them and the questions which she or he is posing. Walter Scott's historical romances are not considered to be secondary sources for they tell us little about the twelfth century; but they are primary evidence for the culture of the late eighteenth and early nineteenth centuries in which he was immersed. They also helped to shape that culture. Similarly John Fowles' *The French Lieutenant's Woman* is a primary source for twentieth-century attitudes to Victorian England. Such is the depth into which some historical novels are researched that we may be tempted to consider them as secondary sources; but even historically authentic novels must be treated with caution.

How can we treat a work of fiction as secondary evidence for the time about which it is written? A novel contains no footnotes, no bibliography, no pretensions to a critical and balanced analysis of sources from which it is drawn, unless one can treat imagination and experience as primary sources. Can one truly call a novel a secondary source in the historical sense of the word? Most novels do not use primary sources, and in the category of historical novels few allow us to examine the sources on which they were based – even the most accurately researched such as Jean Plaidy's Tudor novels. Clearly, even the most accurate historical novel requires corroboration to make it reliable in the historical sense of the word.

Literature and history

If one compares the purpose of history with the novel – even those novels which are written to persuade as well as to entertain – then there are important differences. A novel is a work of fiction; history pretends to deal with actuality. The characters and setting of most novels are imaginary; those of history are 'real' in the sense that they can be located in time as having some existence. And the settings of novels may be challenged as being in some sense fictitious.

History does, however, have some similarities with novels. A.J.P. Taylor described his craft as 'telling a story', and in this he aspires to be like the novelist in claiming literary functions for the historian. Oakeshott went further in likening the historian's activities to the novelist's, arguing that the only explanation of cause and effect should be provided by the story line. When E.M. Forster illustrated the elements of a plot in *English Novel* with reference to two 'facts': 'the king died; the queen died', he was saying something valuable to the historian. He rejected the bald statement of these two facts as being uninteresting and irrelevant to the novelist. He saw that something extra was needed for a plot, that is the ascription of some motive, some interest, some statement about the relationship between these two facts: 'the king died; the queen died of grief'. Similarly, the historian Evans-Pritchard commented, 'History is not a succession of events, it is the links between them.'

Clearly, history, like literature, can be nothing if it deals only with facts. As E. H. Carr points out in *What is History?* historians cannot boast that they know their facts: one would expect no less, but that does not make them historians. Historians, like the novelist, must enter into some dialogue with the facts. They must create some meaning by analysing the relationships between the 'facts'. In this sense they are not far removed from the novelist in that they enter into some sort of dialogue based on their own experience with the material of history. This raises the question of the degree to which imagination and creativity enter into the writing of history and the writing of novels.

Yet, there is a clearly stated difference between history and novels. History is a 'scientific' attempt to re-capture the past, as opposed to the unsystematic attempt to re-create the past in which popular history merges with historical fiction. History must be rooted in evidence which must be evaluated according to a strict methodology before it is accepted into the canon of historical validity. This canon cannot, as Arthur Marwick points out in *The Nature of History*, be created simply because a club of eminent historians lend 'facts' respectability, let alone as an invention of the historian's mind.

However, when one examines the differences more closely one begins to see some blurring of the distinctions between fact and fiction in history and literature. One has to examine more closely the notion of a reality which excludes the truth of novels. Novels are only fictitious in the sense that the events and the characters which they describe usually have no existence outside the mind of the author. But does this mean they are totally fictitious?

Representing historical periods

At the most general level all novels are 'true' in the sense that they deal with the thoughts, feelings, motives and lives of people, and these are rooted in some historical unity of time and space based upon the memory/experience (history) of the author. In a sense they tell us truths about ourselves which have to be validated by references to our experiences as human beings, not to sources; just as the Bible (and all great religious literature) tells us truths about ourselves even in its myths. Their validity is measured against our own attitudes, values and experiences, just as we measure the interpretations of the historian in the light of our own value systems as well as the sources on which they are based.

The absence of source material against which to check the assertions of the novelist does not make novels useless. Novels can be of great use to historians if treated with caution and respect as primary sources. Ordinary novels can tell us much about the culture of the time in which they are set and often more about the times in which they were written as unwitting testimonies. This is particularly important for the creation of meaning which, as Dilthey argued, is essential to understanding internally, as opposed to externally. 'Meaning changes with the period and culture of the historian' (Marwick).

Distorting perceptions?

Dickens for instance gives us a view of Victorian attitudes to the workhouse (*Oliver Twist*), the legal system (*Bleak House*) and economic morality (*Little Dorrit*). If we look more closely at *Oliver Twist* we can see some of the strengths and weaknesses of novels as source material:

> Oliver cried lustily. If he could have known that he was an orphan, left to the tender mercies of the churchwardens, and overseers, perhaps he would have cried the louder.

The historian is here presented with a particular view of the workhouse as a generally undesirable place to be. As Jason Tranter comments:

> The workhouse system is generally perceived in a critical light. The Andover Workhouse Scandal and popular literary work such as *Oliver Twist*, portray the institution as totally inhuman and

barbaric. The radical, caricatured approach adopted by Dickens was used to try and stir the nation's conscience by painting a misleading picture which has remained in the popular mind. This extreme view has been applied generally to the workhouse.

Portsmouth-born Dickens could not have used his local workhouse as a model for *Oliver Twist* because a glance at the Workhouse Visitor's Book suggests that certain standards were maintained. This book is a detailed weekly record of how effectively the workhouse was maintained, of the physical condition and general welfare of the inhabitants, as well as the education of the children. This book had to be presented and inspected at the weekly Board of Guardians meeting. R. Rogers, a local visitor who inspected the premises, reported no information to suggest that conditions were unacceptable: 'examined the provisions and found them very good, particularly the beef, mutton and pork.' On the other hand the practice of picking oakum, described in *Oliver Twist*, is also described in the Portsmouth workhouse. Yet despite the pitfalls here represented by Dickens' novel he does present us with a particular contemporary view of the workhouses two or three years after they began to operate, which must have had some currency among certain sections of English Society.

Insights of the novelist

Similarly, Jane Austen can tell us much about the preoccupations of middle-class Hampshire society, though little about other classes of society; George Eliot gives us a much fuller picture of English Victorian society and culture in *Middlemarch*. In *North and South* and *Mary Barton* Gaskell portrays the Victorian social pyramid, the effects of the Industrial Revolution and Chartism. Chartism is dealt with more specifically in Kingsley's *Alton Locke*. In *Sybil* Disraeli examines the effects on England of 'two nations', whilst D.H. Lawrence's novels present early twentieth-century mining communities and their sexual moralities. Similarly, Fowles can tell us about how twentieth-century writers view Victorian morality in novels such as *The French Lieutenant's Woman*, just as Richardson's *Pamela* is a powerful picture of eighteenth-century social conventions and attitudes to women.

Novels have to be based on experience of character and in settings which are real. This is mediated through the experience of the novelist, but this is precisely what makes it valuable if treated with caution. Why, for example, did Dickens, a middle-class writer who as a ratepayer might be expected to support the workhouse, write in such scathing terms about Oliver Twist's experiences under the New Poor Law? Why did Austen scarcely mention in her novels the Napoleonic Wars raging across the Channel not 40 miles away? What can Forster in his *Maurice*, or Lawrence in *Sons and Lovers* tell us about contemporary attitudes to sexuality?

In studying foreign history Tolstoy's *War and Peace* not only provides us with vivid insights into Russia at war and Napoleon's personality from a Russian point of view, but puts forward theories about the nature of war, historical causation and reasons for Napoleon's defeat. Pasternak's *Doctor Zhivago* provides us with a picture of Russia in revolution from a middle-class point of view. Steinbeck's *The Grapes of Wrath* can tell us much about the effects of Mid-western dustbowls and the sufferings of uprooted families who made their way to the flawed promised land of California to find work. Balzac provides us with a comprehensive picture of French society in the first half of the nineteenth century. Maupassant's short stories provide some keen insights into the culture of France during the period of the Franco-Prussian war. Zola's *Germinal* depicts the life of the nineteenth-century French miner and alerted contemporaries to their terrible working conditions.

Interpretation of the world

Further, novelists, like historians, have world pictures that influence their interpretation of the world. For example, one may see in Walter Scott a romantic view of medieval history, just as one may see in Swift a satirical and cynical attitude to the politics of his times in *Gulliver's Travels*; or in Orwell's *Animal Farm* and *1984*. Novelists, like historians, are coloured by their view of the world and try to persuade us accordingly. In this connection novelists make important – sometimes crucial – contributions to the development of intellectual, or cultural history. For example, Sartre's existentialism is vividly portrayed in *La Nausée* (Nausea), giving us a keen insight into the development of a philosophy rooted in the collapse of France after the occupation of the Nazis and the move away from accepted cultural meanings generally in the first half of the twentieth century. Some of these issues were taken up in Heller's *Catch 22*, which brought the spotlight to bear on the European existentialist view, challenging American conceptions of authority represented in the powerful image of the army by exposing its absurdity.

Novels can also further debates about issues and social conditions: Dostoyevsky's *Crime and Punishment* may be seen as changing people's perceptions of crime, punishment and reparations. *Nicholas Nickleby* and *Jane Eyre* alerted Victorian society to the poor state of public schools. *Lord of the Flies* furthered the twentieth-century pessimist/optimist debate about human nature. Looking again at Russia it is possible to see a powerful connection between Chernyshevsky's novel, *What is to be done?*, Lenin's political development (*What is to be done?*, 1902) and subsequent developments in Russia.

When one moves into the area of the historical novel one can see demonstrated clearly the connection between history and literature. The historical novel does not have a high status among critics of novels. Historical novels are rooted in reality and their plots are ready-made. But the imagination they require is no less than that required for the ordinary novel. Historical novels, like other genres of novel are useful to historians because of their rich empathetic treatment of human motives, emotions, and actions. They 'bring history to life' by creating fully-rounded personae, adding with deft brushstrokes those dimensions which may be missing in the dry history book or the absent source material.

Conclusion

Novels can yield much but they have to be treated with some caution by historians. They have to be corroborated with other sources to check for reliability, typicality, and veracity, or, as Marwick puts it: 'reference has to be made to the society and community in which they lived.' Their fiction has to be checked against historical sources for 'fact'. Their attitudes and values have to be carefully sifted through the accounts of other primary sources. The viewpoint and background of their authors have to be carefully studied. Their ability to persuade and colour has to be carefully balanced against their propaganda function and subjectivity. And in the case of historical novels their possibly facile treatment of historical actualities has to be carefully monitored for myth and distortion. Like the Whig historians of the eighteenth century, or Shakespeare in his plays, novelists have to be carefully assessed to see if they are projecting the values of their own time onto the past; if they are, the angle of approach changes and they are then examined for unwitting insights into their own times. Historians use the novel to 'illustrate', not 'prove' a point, or to 'suggest lines of historical enquiry' (Marwick). If treated with caution, novels can help us get inside an age. In G.M. Young's words, historians must 'read and read until they hear the voices of the age speaking to them'.

Sam Merry is a postgraduate student at Southampton University.

Peter Neville
Examiner's Report

This examiner's report looks at the central question of the ballot in nineteenth-century British history, in an extract format. Students sometimes worry unduly about document questions when they have no need to do so, providing of course they have revised the topic thoroughly.

Question

The Ballot and its Effects

Study Documents 1 and 2 below and then answer questions (a) to i) which follow:

Document 1

The Times newspaper treats the ballot... as a question to be despised and tells us that it is... unmanly to give votes in secret... In a recent Irish election... three men were killed and 28 wounded – such a state exists in no country where the ballot operates... The ballot would make elections tranquil and would withdraw from the landlord... the temptation to... use his tenants' vote to support his own party... If that temptation were withdrawn, you would have more inducement to grant leases to tenants... The ballot is universal in the United States and almost so on the continent of Europe.   line 1

5

10

(John Bright, in a speech made in 1866)

Document 2

It was hoped that the ballot would have put a stop to all corrupt practices... It has only diverted them... The ballot did away with the chance of electors selling cabbages at £10 apiece or a plate of gooseberries for £25 as at Sudbury... and buying up certain houses, granting occupiers a reduction in rent in return for support... This *Corrupt Practices Bill* is a new dispensation... What would the candidates for Yorkshire in 1807, whose joint expenses amounted to just under half a million, say to a bill which enacts the legal expenditure for each candidate must not now exceed £350 for 2000 electors?   15

20

Then as to *treating*... Not many years ago on election morning there were consumed, beside poultry and pastry, 980 stone
of beef, 315 dozen of wine, 72 pipes of ale and 865 gallons of   25
spirit.

Since the Ballot Act, general elections have lost excitement...
The ten days saturnalia of freedom and equality... when tenant
and landlord met on equal terms are no more nor are there   30
showers of cabbage stalks and rotten eggs... Will there be no
more *abduction of voters* and locking them up until after the
election? No hard-fisted supporters of the constitution who
could knock down their political opponents? We are far from   35
the days when the electors of Stratford proposed to their member to introduce a Bill 'for the better payment of voters' – few
will bother to turn out. Mr Trollope, speaking at the election of
1868... remarked, 'political cleanliness was odious to the peo-   40
ple'... We doubt whether the new Bill will eradicate the *habits
of many generations.*

(*Blackwood's Magazine*, **December 1883**)

(a) In the context of these Documents, explain the meanings of:

    (i) 'treating' (line 22); and

    (ii) 'abduction of voters' (line 32)   **(2)**

(b) Analyse, and comment on, the advantages which John Bright predicted in Document 1 would be gained through introducing the
secret Ballot.   **(5)**

(c) To what extent does the author of Document 2 consider that the
results of introducing the Ballot are those which Bright predicted?
What attitudes does this author reveal towards those results?   **(6)**

(d) On what specific point concerning the relationship between land-
lords and tenants is there disagreement between these two writers?   **(2)**

(e) What evidence is supplied by Document 2 of the need for a
'Corrupt Practices Bill' (line 17)?   **(4)**

(f) Taking into account their content and style, which of these two
documents was more in sympathy with the attitudes of the British
public in the second half of the nineteenth century towards the
electoral 'habits of many generations' (lines 41–2)?   **(6)**

Maximum Marks 25

Answers by Barney

(a) (i) Within the context of the documents 'treating' means candidates treated their voters to food and drink. This 'treating' was a form of electoral bribery to gain votes.

(a) (ii) 'Abduction of Voters' meant that gangs of loyal supporters would kidnap opposition voters until the voting was over. This would prevent these voters from casting their vote.

One of the important points to notice about this question is the sub-mark awarded for it (in this case two). Only short relevant answers, are required, and these Barney provides. Avoid the temptation of giving overlong examination answers which use up valuable time.

(b) Many of John Bright's advantages were achieved. The secret ballot did make elections more 'tranquil', violence could no longer be an efficient weapon to be used against voters. because there was no means of distinguishing who voted for whom, thus loyalty could not be proved or disproved. Also for the same reason the Secret Ballot Act did 'withdraw from the Landlord ... the temptation to ... use his tenant's vote to support his own party'. The Landlord could no longer evict his tenants on the grounds of the way they voted. This was because the Landlord could not know how they voted. Bright's claim that 'you would have more inducement to grant leases to tenants' is false. If the Landlord could not influence his tenants he had no reason to grant leases.

This is a good answer. Barney uses part of the extract in his own answer, and this is good technique. He also provides precisely what is asked for and no more. However, candidates who know the history of Irish Home Rule could comment here on the fact that (especially in the light of Bright's remark in line 2) even the secret ballot did not prevent the practice of so called 'personation' when voters would impersonate dead voters.

(c) The author of Document 2 does agree that many of the results of introducing the Ballot were predicted by Bright. Bright wrote 'the Ballot would make elections tranquil' – Document 2 states 'nor are there showers of cabbage stalks and rotten eggs'. Although the author of Document 2 agrees with the changes that Bright predicted, he does not like the changes. The author comments 'general elections have lost excitement ... the ten days saturnalia of freedom and equality'.

Barney contrasts the two extracts quite effectively here. Clearly Blackwood's Magazine *does not like the new tranquil atmosphere in politics likely to come with the passage of the Corrupt Practices Act. One point which he misses is the complaint in Document 2 that one result of the new legislation will be apathy because 'few will bother to turn out' (lines 37–8).The inference here is that democracy will be undermined by the new legislation, although the author's tone is clearly cynical. The lower classes are deemed to be incapable of adjusting to a system where there was no corruption. But was the accusation of likely apathy actually true in the years after 1883? Barney might have commented on the voter turnout in elections after the passing of the act.*

(d) John Bright believed that the secret ballot created equality between tenant and landlord by the ability to 'withdraw from the landlord the temptation to ... use his tenant's vote.' However, the author of Document 2 claims that was their right, he writes 'The ten days Saturnalia of freedom and equality ... when tenant and landlord met on equal terms are no more.'

The answer picks up the difference between Documents 1 and 2 quite well here. However, the point about 'tenant and landlord' meeting on 'equal terms' demands further explanation. Barney notices the different tone in the two extracts, but the question of whether there could ever be real equality under the old system deserves some comment. Again the sub-mark here is only two, so a brief comment will do.

(e) The 'Corrupt Practices Bill' was needed because bribery was still rife. What would the candidates for Yorkshire in 1807, whose joint expenses amounted to just under half a million, say to a Bill which enacts that legal expenditure must not now exceed £350 for 2,000 electors. This shows that the candidates expected to be able to bribe the voters. It claims that the candidates would not be able to get by on just £350 for legal expenses.

Here Barney's answer is not quite full enough. The point about expenses, comparing 1807 with 1883 is made, but the others about 'treating' and the abduction of voters are not. This is unfortunate because four marks are available here for intelligent reading of the text. At best the answer could only expect one mark. This underlines a crucial point about answering document questions. Usually at least half the available marks can be gained by doing nothing more than reading the text carefully. Marks are thrown away with abandon when candidates do not.

(f) Document 1 was more in sympathy with the attitudes of the British public. In the second half of the nineteenth century public opinion was moving away from bribery and electoral expenses. The middle-class voters and later the artisan voters wanted respectable campaigns rather than bribery and corruption. The author of Document 2 is lamenting on the loss of landed interests' total control of parliament, and is not sympathetic to the wants of the new electoral classes. As Bright claimed, elections became more 'tranquil'. Even though the secret ballot did remove many of the landed interests' powers they still commanded a great deal of deference. This deferential voting is referred to in lines 41–2 'we doubt whether the new Bill will eradicate the habits of many generations'.

Two points need to be noted about this final answer. Firstly, six marks are available (as was the case with (c) above). This means that a more lengthy, mini-essay, is required. Secondly, and unlike the other questions, the answer demanded should focus on the wider background to the topic rather than on just the text of extracts. Barney's answer is really too superficial – he is right in his assessment that the first document is more in sympathy with British attitudes, but needs to see the two extracts in the wider perspective of parliamentary reform since 1832. Since that date there had been a steady increase in the size of the electorate, culminating in the 1884 Act which followed the Corrupt Practices Act (although it would be pertinent to point out that universal male suffrage came only in 1918, and universal female suffrage in 1928). Hence Blackwood's Magazine *seems to be fighting against the historical tide in its attitudes. After all, Charles Dickens was an extremely popular contemporary novelist who lampooned British Parliamentary practice in the* Pickwick Papers. *It is because he hasn't developed his answers quite enough, that Barney would only get a respectable grading for this answer rather than a good one. He makes the right judgements but needs more evidence either from the extracts, or from his own knowledge, to back them up.*

Peter Neville is an A-level examiner and author of *Neville Chamberlain* **in the Hodder and Stoughton** *'Personalities and Power'* **series.**